PREPARING
FOR YOUR
CIVIL
DEPOSITION

A GUIDE FOR THE
LAW ENFORCEMENT PROFESSIONAL

George T. Williams

CUTTING EDGE
TRAINING

Bellingham, Washington, USA

A Cutting Edge Training Book

PUBLISHED BY CUTTING EDGE TRAINING, LLC

Preparing For Your Civil Deposition:
A Guide for the Law Enforcement Professional
Copyright 2013 by George T. Williams. All rights reserved.

Cover Design by: Rod Burton
Cover Image by: khz - Fotolia.com

Printed in the United States of America.

Cutting Edge Training utilizes print on demand publishing to conserve natural resources, reduce overstocking, warehousing, and unnecessary waste.

ISBN: 978-0615965260

What the experts are saying about this book:

"Gordon Graham here with a quick tip for you regarding the importance of a civil deposition. Over the forty years I have been associated with law enforcement I have had scores of Officers/Deputies/Troopers not appreciate the "risk" involved in a deposition. Allow me to give you a big hint—a deposition is a big deal, and if not taken seriously can lead to all sorts of bad results. The plaintiff lawyer (the guy suing you) recognizes the value of this deposition—he/she is probably the person who asked for it! They know that a lot of cops are not prepared for this deposition (oral examination under oath) because the cop is more concerned about the upcoming trial. My personal belief is that this lack of preparation is the cause for many unfortunate outcomes including settlements and verdicts. So I encourage you to get a copy of George Williams' book on this important topic "Preparing for Your Civil Deposition" (how he came up with this title is a mystery) and read it now and read it again if you ever get sued. There is a 50% chance you will be sued in your law enforcement career so this is something you need to be concerned with. I have known George for thirty years and his work in preparing cops physically and mentally for the risks involved in cop work is outstanding. For the price of a couple of energy drinks you can do something now to prevent big problems in the future."

> **Gordon Graham**, JD. *California Highway Patrol (Commander, retired), International public risk management consultant and highly sought after presenter and trainer.*

"A long-overdue book that every Cop needs. Easy to read, yet full of valuable info that will help you to protect yourself in court. Don't get deposed without it!"

> **Steve Ashley**. *MS, MLS, MFCI, MUFI, ARM-P, CLS2. Risk manager, expert witness, author, and international training consultant.*

"Training for cops to prevail in deadly force encounters has been available for years. What has been painfully missing is training for cops to prevail in the legal fights they are more likely to face than shootings. This book provides that training. Every cop should read this and every civil defense attorney should make sure his or her cop reads it before a deposition."

> **Jeff Martin**, JD. ARM. *San Jose (CA) Police Department, (Sergeant, retired), expert witness, and national police trainer.*

"Mr. George Williams is a formable expert in the field of police force litigation. George provides valuable insight into the realm of preparing for and providing depositions, which is attributed to his decades of work in this field. Without a doubt all ranks in law enforcement will benefit from this body of work, especially those facing deposition. George's unwavering and selfless mentorship throughout the years has made me the police supervisor and trainer I am today."

> **Craig Allen**. *Sergeant, Hillsboro (OR) Police Department, expert witness, and national police trainer.*

Also by George T. Williams:

Force Reporting for Every Cop

Praise for *Force Reporting for Every Cop*:

Force Reporting for Every Cop should have been written long ago. There is no doubt it could have saved many officers and saved their agencies a lot of money in legal expenses or expert witness fees. George's text is designed to be an off-the-shelf reference book that will benefit every cop who works the street.

George includes sample Force Response Narrative Reports and a checklist for your own reports. Some officers may wish to change the terminology or alter the language to fit their agency's needs, but the important thing is to adopt the philosophy of comprehensively reporting your response to the subject's actions. And that is where the real value in *Force Reporting for Ever Cop* is realized. Enjoy it. Learn from it. Use it.

> **Dave Grossi**. *Former Lead Instructor, Calibre Press, Inc., Street Survival Seminars, expert witness, national police trainer.*

Admonishment and Waiver:

This book is not intended to be legal advice. The author is not an attorney, and the information provided is not a substitute for professional legal advice and services. If you require or desire legal assistance, please seek out the services of a competent professional. The author, publisher, and their employees and agents are not liable for any damages arising from or in connection with the use of or reliance on any information contained this book.

Because of the dynamic nature of the internet, any web addresses or links contained in this book may have changed since publication and may no longer be valid.

Dedication

This book would not have been possible without the assistance of my best friend in this world, my lovely bride, Cynthia. It is her patient editing and relentless drive to create the best possible product we are able to for those who risk everything they have to protect people who are unknown to them. I am immeasurably grateful to her for being my wife and business partner. God sure smiled upon me for some unknown reason.

I also want to thank Attorney Jeff Martin (retired sergeant San Jose, California, Police Department and certified risk manager) for his vetting the contents of the book. Jeff has been a great friend for many, many years, and I am grateful for his kind, supportive, and critical assistance with this work.

Finally, I am grateful for every attorney I have worked for and against for the wide experience I have been granted in my career as an expert witness. Sometimes the experience has been great, and other times humbling, but I have learned something from every one of them. And I hope to pass on these learnings to those officers who have achieved proper conduct, who have upheld their oath, who have risked their safety and lives to protect others, and who are now being called upon to answer in the courts for their actions.

***

Contents

Introduction

If you're reading this book, it's likely you have been served with a subpoena ordering you to provide deposition testimony. Realizing you are about to enter into an unfamiliar and decidedly hostile process, you are smart enough to know you need some education about the deposition process and how you can increase the likelihood of your success. After all, you believe your career—and even personal finances—might be at stake.

In defending your actions in civil court, you will be required to prove that you preserved the rights of the suspect—who is now suing you as the Plaintiff—just as you are required to justify following every contact and enforcement action. In cases where you responded with force, you will be required to prove that you met the "reasonable officer standard." How you accomplished the arrest and took the subject into custody will be analyzed detail-by-micro-detail by attorneys and their experts who represent the Plaintiff. All force and any other intrusion into the subject's life may be an element of this lawsuit against you, including the tactics and methods you employed.

Providing deposition testimony is a straight forward process. Opposing attorney(s) will ask you questions and you will provide answers under oath. This question and answer exercise will likely encompass the details of your background, training, and experience. It will, without doubt, go into great detail about your observations and actions prior to, during, and following the incident in question. Seems simple enough, right? Many officers, experienced in criminal court testimony, think they can just "wing it." And many do just that with widely mixed and often disappointing results.

This book is the result of over two decades of my defending officers in civil and criminal courts throughout the country as an expert witness. I've been up against the best of the plaintiffs' bar while also having the privilege of working for some of the finest attorneys who defend officers. This experience includes reading, digesting, and synthesizing hundreds upon hundreds of depositions given by officers in litigation alleging police misconduct. Their deposition testimony was taken in many cases by litigators who are experts in the business at winning police misconduct cases and separating agencies from their budgets. Although infrequent, officers' may be penalized by having to pay out of their personal assets.

The information in this book is also based upon the advice of some of the best police civil defense attorneys in the business. Without exception, officers who prepare well for their depositions tend to do well facing even the best attorneys, and thus assist in the defense of their cases. Those who fail to ready themselves rarely do as well, and sometimes literally lose what was a winnable case for themselves and their agencies by giving terrible deposition testimony. The result and effectiveness of deposition testimony is largely up to the officer.

This is a whole new testimony environment for you. Regardless of how well or how often you have testified as a criminal prosecution witness, civil court is a wholly different environment. There is a necessary depth of testimony that takes you to a wholly new level of questioning of your job knowledge and training, your actions, and even your thoughts during the incident. This examination may tax your capabilities in describing in detail the threat the suspect posed to yourself, other officers, and/or to the public, and why you acted reasonably in the face of that threat.

The information in this book was hard won by officers who did the job properly on the street, and were then rewarded with a lawsuit. Don't let this part of being a cop victimize you. Our system is one in which the police are policed by the citizens who take time out of their busy lives to perform a duty that few humans in history have ever experienced: sitting in judgment as a juror of those individuals who are the enforcement arm of their government. Without this system, policing in North America would not be a profession with its current high standards, and might remain little different than Third World countries where police do little more than prey upon their populace.

That you will uphold the oath you took when you accepted your badge as well as the oath you take in court to give truthful testimony goes without saying. Whatever the fact pattern your particular case might entail, this book will help prepare you to meet the challenge of providing accurate, comprehensive testimony against the top-tier litigators. However, it can't and won't help you if you don't put in the required sweat equity. Like most things in life, the higher the quality of your effort in implementing a smart plan, the more likely it will pay off for you.

In some parts of this book, case law has been cited to illustrate or better explain the suggested articulation point. Be advised that it is prudent to do your own research as case law and legislative requirements change. Staying current with your policy and both state and federal case law is vital both to your effectiveness as an officer and as a high quality witness. A glossary of terms has been provided.

There are language realities that any author must address when writing a piece involving both genders. As a life-long police trainer, I recognize that women play a beneficial role in policing in North America. They, too, are and will be defendants who need to prepare for their day in court. In the writing of this work, I have elected to stay with the male pronoun for ease of reading and in the hope of increasing the understandability of the work. While there are excellent female civil defense attorneys as well as formidable female plaintiffs' attorneys, it is easier in the writing and the reading not to have to switch back and forth, or to use the "s/he, him/her, he/she" variations. Until someone comes up with a universal non-gender-specific human-pronoun, we'll just have to stay with the male pronoun, and continue to bear with disclaimers such as these.

While this book was written for the police officer who is being sued for taking some sort of law enforcement action, the content is appropriate for any person who is a party to a lawsuit and is soon to provide deposition testimony. If you are not a cop, take what is valuable to you and disregard the rest. Any witness who is being deposed will benefit from the knowledge of the process derived from Chapters One and Four.

Wandering through this civil-litigation wilderness without a guide can be detrimental to many aspects of your life. That's the reason for this book; so that good officers who reasonably do the job the way they are trained and who put themselves in harm's way for others can have a step-by-step process to prepare for their day in court. The first step in this (beyond the initial reporting which cannot be rewritten or re-interviewed) is the deposition testimony. Prepare well. It is worth it to you, your family, your agency, and to law enforcement in general. God bless you for the work you do and the sacrifices you make on behalf of us all.

Stay safe on the street, and good luck in your case.

George T. Williams
Bellingham, WA
June, 2013

CHAPTER ONE

Orienting to Your New Reality

"It" happened. You were served some time ago with a Summons informing you that you are now a "defendant" in a civil rights lawsuit. Your case may be heard separately in federal court, state court, or a federal court may hear both the federal and state actions combined. It may have resulted from an incident involving some type of force, perhaps even a deadly force response. Most often, however, it is the result of something fairly low-level and may not involve significant injury to anyone at all. In fact, it is not uncommon to see lawsuits filed against officers when the subject was merely detained in handcuffs for a few minutes with no subsequent arrest. When you were served, you may not have remembered the name of the suspect-now-plaintiff who is suing you. After all, it's been two to three years and how many hundreds of detentions and arrests have you conducted since then? But you know the Plaintiff's name now, and you will be required to answer his allegations and prove your proper conduct based on your reasonable perceptions of his behavior.

The administrative investigation is long in the past, and you were probably cleared of any wrongdoing by the Internal Affairs/Professional Standards unit of your agency. Your incident may be one where the suspect was injured or perhaps detained for only a few minutes, leading to findings of "exonerated" or "not sustained" by your agency. If you were involved in a deadly force response, you've already been through that wringer, probably including interview(s) by homicide investigators from within your agency and District Attorney's investigators. Depending on local practices, a Coroner's Inquest and/or grand jury might be convened to evaluate the case for potential criminal charges against you. Months later (sometimes even more than a year post-incident), you finally received an official letter ruling the shooting as "justified." While there was no question in your mind and that of your peers, there was still that sense of relief when you were notified that it was finally over, lifting that pressing weight off your chest you almost took for granted.

Then the Summons arrived. And now there's that weight pressing in your chest again, the one you thought was gone forever. You may find yourself thinking about the incident more and more.

By now, you have already met with your civil attorney. Whether this individual is employed by your city attorney's, state's attorney's or county counsel's office; or is a private attorney hired by your jurisdiction, you may have already conferred with him several times. Hopefully, your attorney is an experienced police specialist who understands your job, tactics, and your agency's policies, as well as the laws governing the force response by police. Both of you should have already been over the case and the factual basis of your state of mind as well as the justifications for your actions. You and your attorney have worked out your defense strategy. Interrogatories (sworn written answers to written questions during civil discovery; in some states they are called "written depositions") have been completed and signed some time ago.

Your attorney's administrative assistant may have recently contacted you and asked if you would be available for a deposition on any of the dates she provided. The Plaintiff's attorney may have served you with a subpoena ordering you to appear. That subpoena generally will have come through your usual agency channels. If the opposing attorney is a bully, he may have you served at your home in front of your family for the sole purpose of upsetting everyone, adding to the stress of what is generally an already uncertain situation. This is intended as an intimidation tactic, to send a message to you that "nowhere is safe." It's all right…take a breath. He just let you know what kind of attorney—and person—he is. Information is power, and now you know more about him than you did before.

A deposition? You are probably figuring, "OK. I'll handle it." So you cleared the day with your supervisor and you plan to report promptly to the location of the deposition as scheduled. If you are like many officers, your attitude and self-talk runs something like this:

> "A deposition where I have to testify about the case? Hey…It's no big deal. I did nothing wrong and have nothing to hide. I did a good job. Besides, I testify in traffic court all the time, and sometimes in criminal court. I'll just show up, tell them what happened, and get this done. It's all good…"

Except it may not be "all good." While you may have testified in several criminal trials—you may even be a specialist in criminal testimony—and frequently in traffic court, a civil trial is a different animal. You will soon be testifying within a different context. That context can be summarized by the following:

- **The deposition.** A "deposition" is testimony given under oath in an informal setting. This sworn question and answer session carries the same weight, responsibilities, and consequences as your testimony in open court. The rules governing what may be asked of you are different than in court, and the deposition generally results in a much more thorough questioning of your actions, beliefs, and observations than you have ever experienced in prior testimony.

- **First and foremost, you are the "defendant."** This is unfamiliar territory for you. As a part of the criminal prosecution, you are accustomed to automatically being the "good guy" serving the public's welfare by arresting criminals and attempting to gain the conviction of the guilty for their commission of crimes. Regardless of the "innocent until proven guilty" rules of US courts, human nature being what it is, the average juror often assumes the defendant is accused of a crime for a reason.

As the defendant in the civil trial, you will likely run into this very same assumption by the jurors deciding your case. Everyone in the courtroom knows he or she is in that courtroom because you are accused of violating the civil rights of the Plaintiff(s). Additionally, the public is bombarded with isolated negative images of law enforcement by the news media. Hollywood promulgates fictional events of excessive force and wrongdoing by individual officers and law enforcement in general as if it were the norm rather than the rare event that makes it "news" or entertainment. Rarely will you be accused of simply making a mistake that led to the injury or loss. Rather, nine times out of ten, defendant officers are accused of being "thugs," "acting maliciously," and "intentionally inflicting harm" on the plaintiffs they arrested. This plays into a juror's expectation shaped by the news media's and Hollywood's constant portrayal of law enforcement as sadistic and crooked that in no way accurately reflects your life and job. It is something you will have to overcome through your bearing and accurate testimony.

- **A different type of testimony.** Testimony in criminal cases is often very superficial regarding your own actions and behavior because the focus is on whether or not the criminal defendant committed the criminal acts he is accused of. It is not unusual for an arresting officer to spend less than thirty minutes testifying about everything having to do with a "force" case. This usually includes developing probable cause, the detention and/or arrest, how the criminal defendant resisted arrest, and what force the officer reacted with to overcome that resistance or assault.

In civil trial, the testimony is quite different. You will be asked to provide a moment-by-moment accounting of your entire part in the incident.

In civil trial, the testimony is quite different. You will be asked to provide a moment-by-moment accounting of your entire part in the incident. Everything regarding your actions, your beliefs, your observations, the justification for everything you did/thought/knew/were or were not trained to do is subject to examination. It is not unusual for a defendant officer to testify for three to six hours—or more— on an arrest that took no more than ten minutes from contact to handcuffs and a force response of less than a minute

A good opposing attorney will attempt to put you on the defensive and keep you there throughout your testimony.

resulting in minor bruising and a scrape or two. Two and three days of testimony are not unheard of in some more involved cases.

A good opposing attorney will attempt to put you on the defensive and keep you there throughout your testimony. Some will play lawyer's games, attempting to get you to admit points that seem oh-so-silly at the moment but may be cumulative in the minds of jurors. The best of them will bring every scrap of prior testimony in the present case, as well as your previous testimony in other cases, in an attempt to impeach your credibility and impugn your veracity. It is normal for you to be asked detailed questions about the testimony you provided in the original criminal trial of the Plaintiff, and you should prepare for it.

- **A different degree of motivation and preparation by opposing counsel.** The amount of time and the intensity of preparation by opposing counsel in a civil case will be unlike anything you have experienced in your previous criminal testimony—even against the best criminal defense lawyers (unless you were involved in the OJ Simpson trial and his $10 million defense "Dream Team"). The criminal defense attorneys you have been up against generally spend little time with a particular case to maximize their busy client schedule. They are often juggling far too many cases to be intimately familiar with all of the facts—and there is typically far less information available to the criminal attorney than there is for a civil case. It is not unusual for a criminal defense attorney—especially an overworked public defender—to have read the case once or twice, met a couple of times with their client, and then appear in court to answer "ready" to present a defense at trial in front of a jury.

Plaintiffs' attorneys have a completely different orientation to the civil trial. Commonly, they are working on a contingency basis. They are paid only if they win, and this case may represent a total of three to six months of pay for them. Look in the mirror and ask yourself, "How hard would I prepare for a week-long trial if my next six months of income solely depended upon winning?"

If they win:

o   In state court, they get a percentage of the judgment against your jurisdiction.

o   In federal court, they are awarded "reasonable attorney fees" as the "prevailing party." These are often *very* lucrative, and can be much more than the plaintiff is awarded. These awards can range up to six figures.

As such, the Plaintiff's attorney you are facing will typically have a mastery of every detail of the witness statements and interviews (including any involved officers, other police witnesses, the Plaintiff, involved witnesses, and uninvolved witnesses), the evidence, your training and personnel history, your report(s) and interviews. Plaintiffs' attorneys are often mistaken regarding how you are trained and are expected to operate in the real world to resolve the problems you encounter as an officer. However, they are generally articulate and impassioned, and will challenge you on every action and decision for its legal and tactical validity. This will be especially true for any of your actions that would create the slightest doubt of the reasonableness of your actions and decision making.

•   **Expert consultation.** Expert witnesses are generally former police officers who have no loyalty or love for you. They advise plaintiffs' attorneys on any perceived weaknesses in your testimony or tactics. These experts often are formerly high ranking—it is not unusual for them to have been commanders, assistant chiefs, deputy chiefs, and chiefs of police of both medium and large agencies. Many also have a long list of training courses attended, credentials, and education.

This expert will assist the Plaintiff's attorney in developing a strategy for challenging your conduct, behavior, and actions during the detention and/or arrest of their client. They often invent what they represent to be "national standards of conduct" for police. Many of these experts purport dubious, almost comical assertions of "national standards for proper tactics and restraints" by officers. Here are just a few examples of some of these unbelievable assertions (with straight faces and under oath):

o   Officers should use a blanket to defend against a knife-wielding suspect charging out of a bedroom at them by wrapping him up in the cloth without the need to shoot the suspect or use a TASER: "Just like we used to do before we had these out of control cops today."

o   Officers should have the ability to "talk down" a mentally ill subject in the middle of psychotic break or who is under the influence of drugs (or both) and is non-communicative. In fact, according to them, it seems to be pretty simple to accomplish if you just care about people as much as they did when they were a cop on the mean streets. According to their testimony: "I used to do it all the time. Heck, we all did. These officers today just don't know how to talk to people and they are too quick to resort to force…"

o   Officers should never put their weight on the combative suspect's chest or back when he is on the ground because "everyone knows that kills people." They will earnestly testify, "Doing that is just like murdering the Plaintiff's husband."

Their high rank and education unfortunately gives them credibility in front of juries. For example, in a case involving two police officers dealing with a mentally ill man moving angrily with a tire iron upraised at one officer from less than ten feet away, the former high-ranking old gentleman acting as an expert on behalf of the plaintiffs authoritatively asserted that a tire iron is not considered to be a deadly weapon. The officers should have simply put their handguns away, split up, and maneuvered with one officer moving to the suspect's front with the other officer to his back. The officers should then have "tackled" the subject without injury to anybody.

From the juror's perspective, if an individual of such rank, education, and tenure in law enforcement testifies against the defendant officers, it casts doubt that these officers were reasonable in their conduct.

He further opined, "There is no need to shoot someone who is simply trying to hit you with a tire iron. That's how my partner and I would have done it." Jurors just didn't know that they should be laughing in derision, be affronted at such testimony under oath, or, perhaps, be throwing rotting vegetables at this expert on the stand. From the juror's perspective, if an individual of such rank, education, and tenure in law enforcement testifies against the defendant officers, it casts doubt that these officers were reasonable in their conduct.

Plaintiffs' experts tend to use a "shotgun" approach in making numerous assertions of impropriety, illegal conduct, improper tactics, and apparent lack of training. The expert is certain the officer acted with malice, deliberate disregard, and with indifference to the plaintiff's civil rights. Regardless of your perception of the absurdity and outrageousness of this expert's assertions—and you will likely think it all of that and more—you will be required to answer and explain in detail why the actions you responded with were reasonable, trained, and commonly employed by officers in your agency, region, state, and nation.

About Police Civil Defense Attorneys

Some police civil defense attorneys are masters of their craft. If they are not, they tend not to last in this area of legal practice. Most are average to above-average attorneys striving to do the job well. The vast majority I've worked for are honest and forthright. Only a couple were people I would never work for again.

One of the first things you want to look for in your attorney is how well he prepares you for your part in the case.

- Did he meet with you soon after you were served with the summons to discuss the case? Ideally, he set up a meeting with you as soon as he was assigned to your case. He likely had spoken to someone in your command staff about you and the case prior to this meeting. This meeting was his first chance to see if what was reported to him was accurate, and to evaluate you as a defendant. If you haven't had this meeting yet, remember to read your report several times prior to the meeting to refresh your memory. It's probably been two years or more since you thought about the case.

- Had your attorney already read your reports? Was he able to intelligently discuss the facts with you? It is reassuring to walk into a meeting where so much depends upon his ability to represent the facts of the case and have him prepared to discuss your actions and perceptions.

- How much time has been spent discussing the case and the strategy he will likely use? Good attorneys will put in serious time with their defendant officers. Preparations may take anywhere from 30-50 hours prior to the deposition. This may include going to the scene, as well as group discussions with all of the involved-defendants as well as witness officers.

- Does he know anything about your job beyond what the average viewer will have learned from one too many episodes of *Cops*? Some in-house attorneys have multiple responsibilities as your jurisdiction's attorney. On Mondays, they draft zoning ordinances. On Tuesdays, they work on a dispute over fencing and city/county property. On

Wednesdays, they deal with contracts. On Thursdays, they are involved in litigation about road design. On Friday, they put on their police-litigation hat. The fact is, police force law is either just touched upon in law school, or ignored altogether. It is a significant area of law that attorneys must learn about on their own.

- Is your attorney up to date on the science of human factors and performance limitations? As you know, there is more to being a police officer than case law when it comes to surviving the street. Humans, by design, are limited in their abilities to perceive, interpret and react to threats, not to mention seeing and remembering everything in a dynamic, time-compressed, highly adrenalized, and threatening event. As the human inside the uniform, what you realistically can, and more importantly, cannot do, when under threat is a major factor in the reasonableness of your actions. At present, the best source of information about police-specific human factors is the Force Science Institute (www.forcescience.org). You should make your attorney aware of this invaluable resource if he isn't already.

The more your attorney understands your job, the dynamic nature of the event, and the time-is-life sensitivity of your perceptions, the better he will be able to assist you in your defense.

The bottom line is that it may be up to you to assist in getting your attorney sufficiently familiarized with what he needs to know about your job and your side of the facts. The more your attorney understands your job, the dynamic nature of the event, and the time-is-life sensitivity of your perceptions, the better he will be able to assist you in your defense. Most attorneys really care about their job and want to ably represent their clients. Ensure your attorney understands what your training was, and how your actions and behavior comported with your policies and practices in daily policing. Importantly, ensure he understands how your actions and decisions are commonplace and something another officer would have done if put in the same situation.

About Plaintiffs' Attorneys

Plaintiffs' attorneys come in all shapes, sizes, and genders. They range from incredibly brilliant attorneys who are fearsome in their ability to twist your testimony and create confusion, to individuals who cause you to scratch your head and wonder how they graduated from high school, much less passed the bar exam. While the best may seem nearly clairvoyant in their abilities, most are just average attorneys with average skills. Still, an average attorney is someone who is competent at his job and should not be taken lightly by any non-attorney (e.g., *you*) stepping onto their turf and entering into their game.

With that said, plaintiffs' attorneys are often built up in the minds of officers as dreaded, all-powerful creatures. This generally results from police instructors and administrators with little or no experience in civil liability prevention constantly talking about the dreaded and extremely ominous "liability," and issuing non-stop warnings of universal catastrophe, such as "You're gonna get sued and lose your house if you…(do anything)!" Some police officers have created such a picture of doom in their minds they become functionally ineffective during their deposition testimony, and act out a self-fulfilling prophecy of their fears. Most, however, are simply nervous. They tend to calm down within five minutes and those who prepare well are able to give their best testimony.

Some plaintiffs' attorneys are simply working for their client, and some may even believe their client's version of the case, at least at the beginning of the case. Many are "true believers" who are convinced that while they may or may not have begun the job as bad people, officers are almost universally thuggish liars. A proportion of these plaintiffs' attorneys actually hate the police and all they stand for. These individuals tend to believe that every officer is an enthusiastic participant in the "Code of Silence" and that any similarity between two officers' accounts of a case is proof positive of collusion and conspiracy. A few are extremely political and became police litigation specialists to do their part to "destroy the Machine (the U.S. government, capitalism, etc.) from within." And almost all are suing in federal court because the attorney's fees awarded by the court can be very lucrative.

One thing that is universal among plaintiffs' attorneys is that they are motivated. They are driven to win and to prove you wrong. They gain their income from that win while affirming their beliefs in the validity of their individual causes and beliefs. As such, there will be no slack or mercy. They will exploit every weakness you offer to them, particularly where your lack of readiness results in less than accurate or inconsistent testimony.

It is your preparation, combined with your ability to clearly explain your actions and reasoning, that will likely determine whether or not the deposition is successful for your case. Strive for perfection in your testimony, and accept nothing less than an excellent deposition. Forget being frightened of the opposing counsel. You have the facts on your side, and, by following the preparation steps as suggested in this book, your readiness will be at its peak because you have done your homework.

"I have a feeling we're not in Kansas anymore…"

As a police specialist—a skilled first responder and investigator who is secure in the mastery of your force tools and tactics—you are competent to handle what comes up in the street. You are the professional in your arena, an investigative force to be reckoned with by the criminal element, a master of assisting the weak and innocent, and an expert at solving fast-moving, highly dangerous problems where lives literally are in the balance. You take charge at the scene until the suspect fails to cooperate. And you then, within the law, force the suspect to comply with your directives. You are like a falcon, a master of his environment, swooping in to protect and serve, using your cop's eyes to spot evil-doing suspects, and willing to put your life on the line to protect the weak and innocent.

Your world vis-à-vis the present court proceeding is much different, however. You are now the defendant—a position of distinct disadvantage in a courtroom. Your police skills and tactics are as valuable to you in this new venue as a falcon's when twenty feet under water.

As the defendant in a civil lawsuit, it is vital to understand this fact: you are now in the domain of attorneys, people who live and die grounded in their abilities to win their cases. Their weapons and tactics are carefully chosen words, artful phrases, and clever arguments. As skilled as you are in your world, this legal professional may be as skilled and experienced in his. And he is hungry.

More than one officer has flippantly believed that he could "handle" the deposition based on his normal criminal witness and testimony expertise. Walking into the deposition with this attitude, perhaps having read his report

While lawyers say, "Bad facts make bad case law," often the reality is "Reasonable facts poorly articulated make bad case law."

"once a couple of weeks ago" often results, at best, in a lackluster performance that is not helpful to the officer's defense. At worst, that testimony will lose the case for both the officer and the agency, outrage the jury, and create the belief that he must be taught a lesson as an example to law enforcement as a whole to dissuade this type of "misconduct" in the future. It may also result in everyone knowing this officer's actions and behavior in the case of "Smith v. (OFFICER'S NAME HERE)" where his agency and maybe even the officer was hit with an astronomical adverse judgment. While lawyers say, "Bad facts make bad case law," often the reality is "Reasonable facts poorly articulated make bad case law."

It is vital for you to understand a simple, universal truth about depositions, civil trials, criminal trials, administrative investigations, and every situation in which you find yourself as a police officer:

> *In court, it doesn't matter that you did a good job on the street. It only matters that you are able to prove that you did a good job on the street.*

You need to hear this again. The ability to prove your case is as important as having reasonably acted in the street. It is the second half of any good detention or arrest. If you can't prove your proper conduct, you will experience an adverse judgment and the frustration and outrage of being publicly judged to be incompetent, or maybe even worse. Additionally, *although unlikely*, the jury has the ability to impose "punitive penalties" making you personally liable for the amount of the punitive judgment against you. These "punitives" may or may not be covered by your jurisdiction, and you may be required to personally pay the judgment to the Plaintiff.

As a criminal investigator and prosecutorial witness, you have likely been trained to believe that once the booking process is completed, the trial and your testimony against the criminal defendant in trial is the most important activity in the legal process. Criminally that may be true from an officer's standpoint, but the civil process is far different. Every bit of evidence you have given, collected, or testified to in this case, as well as similar prior cases in which you were involved may be sieved for information, omissions, and contradictions. Each stage of the civil case must be consistently and comprehensively detailed. The more consistent and thorough your testimony, from your initial report to your final testimony in court, the more likely you will have a verdict you can be proud of.

"Context" is King

The ability to put your actions, decisions, and behavior into context will mean the difference between a favorable or adverse verdict. Detentions, arrests, force responses—even those resulting in the death of someone you mistook as armed—are justifiable only within a narrow context of understanding, actions, behavior, and time. Failing to appreciate this fact and giving sloppy testimony by not ensuring that your answers are in the context of what you knew at the time of your contact with the Plaintiff—especially to questions having constitutional consequences—can be extremely bad for you and the outcome of your case.

"Context" is aptly summed up in that famous phrase that every officer knows but may not appreciate how very important it is in articulating and justifying his actions: "...based on the totality of the facts and circumstances known to the officer at the time." This is not just some random phrase added to what seems like nearly every other paragraph in case law decisions involving a police force response. Rather, it is a requirement for officers, attorneys, judges, and juries to consider the *context* of the circumstances in which the officer was acting.

In a court room, the jury will be instructed not to consider the actual facts known after the incident to be involved in the case. They will, rather, be directed to deliberate only upon what was reasonably perceived and believed by the officer despite the outcome. Being human, 20/20 hindsight is natural to the juror, especially when led to it through every utterance of the plaintiff's attorney and his witnesses. In all actuality, the problem is not so much 20/20 *hindsight* but 20/20 *foresight.* Knowing the outcome of an event, e.g., the suspect is dead after being shot by the defendant officer, leads to a natural but incorrect conclusion that the events leading to the shooting were predictable and the officer therefore has some culpability if his tactics or behavior was not superlative.

> *"Context" is aptly summed up in that famous phrase that every officer knows but may not appreciate how very important it is in articulating and justifying his actions: "...based on the totality of the facts and circumstances known to the officer at the time."*

Most of the time when you receive a call for service, there is nothing about it that would lead you to believe that this is THE CALL where you will be forced to defend your life. As you park, as you approach, as you contact the subject, as you develop reasonable suspicion, as you attempt to detain, as you develop probable cause to arrest, and then attempt to make that arrest, you have no clue that you are about to be forced to shoot that person—until it happens. If you could have predicted it before you realized there was an imminent threat to your life, you probably would have done something else, but the suspect's decision to attempt to murder you changed the equation. Our minds perceive causation because that is how we make sense of the world. Think of a game of pool, where the cue ball strikes the "four" ball, which in turn strikes the "seven" ball which then hits the "eight" ball, *causing* it to fall into the corner pocket.

Causation is convenient in many contexts, but it is generally an error in the evaluation of the reasonableness of an officer's force. In truth, it is the suspect's decisions, his actions and behavior that *cause* an officer's reasonable force response, not the actions of an officer leading up to the force. This is why the Graham Court required the evaluation be from the officer's state of mind, rather than the facts as proven by the later investigation.

The context of the case presented to the jury is about putting them into your shoes at the time you were involved in the event.

The context of the case presented to the jury is about putting them into your shoes *at the time* you were involved in the event. That is your job, accomplished through your comprehensive testimony about your reasonable perceptions at the time. Without your testimony providing your context for the jury, they will arrive at someone else's version of the facts and that will not be good for your case.

"Excessive force" is presently defined as "Force which cannot be justified in light of all of the circumstances known to the officer at the time."[1] Let's break this down into its component parts in order to better understand what this means in your practical world, both as an officer and a civil defendant:

- "Justified." In this context, justification means the ability to "articulate" your actions in response to the suspect's behavior and acts. It is the ability to explain in a manner that makes your proper conduct apparent to others. Are you able to prove that the force options and duration with which you responded met the "reasonable officer standard?" That is,

---

[1] Black's Law Dictionary.

"[w]ould another officer with similar training and experience, given the same or similar situation, respond in the same way or make the same decision?"[2] To "prove" something, one must make the facts plain to someone other than himself.

- "In light of all the circumstances known to you at the time." This is, simply, everything you knew, learned, or observed before and during the incident that you relied upon to make the decisions affecting the outcome of the event. The list of possible facts and circumstances that might be a factor in your decision-making is infinite. However, a brief list might include:

  o The reasonable perception of the conduct of the suspect.

  o Officer/subject factors: variances in size, weight, relative strength, apparent training, injury to or exhaustion of the officer, number of officers to the number of suspects, etc.

  o If the suspect was under the influence of drugs or alcohol, or was apparently, or known to be, mentally ill.

  o The armed status of the suspect (or the proximity of weapons).

  o Potential injury to civilians, children, other officers, or to the arresting officer.

  o The risk of escape.

  o Any exigent circumstances.[3]

Based on this definition and understanding of excessive force, if you are unable to explain the context in which you contacted, detained and/or arrested the subject, and how you responded with force to defend yourself or others, effect that arrest,

---

[2] California POST Basic Course Workbook Series, Learning Domain 20, 2009. Page 16.

[3] This list was derived from Attorney Bruce D. Praet's force policy which later became the foundation for Policy 300 of the Lexipol policy manual. www.lexipol.com.

overcome resistance, or prevent the escape of the subject, your actions will be considered excessive and thus an unconstitutional violation of the Plaintiff's rights. The more context you provide, the more likely your actions, decisions, and force response(s) (if any) will be found to be reasonable and justified. This can include, but is definitely not limited to:

- The facts that you understood from the initial dispatch (whether by radio, cell phone, or via your mobile computer), as well as subsequent updates from either dispatchers or fellow officers prior to arrival.

- Any prior information you knew about the situation or involved parties.

- If the event was an "on-view" crime, the factors alerting you to the likelihood of a crime being committed.

- The facts you received from the Reporting Party(ies).

- The information given to you by the suspect, as well as your observation of his behavior, attitude, and conduct.

- The signs of the subject being under the influence of alcohol or drugs, or possibly being mentally ill.

- Where the event took place, including the physical layout, witnesses and their behavior.

- How the suspect's conduct caused you to fear for your safety, forcing you to respond with force.

- Your injuries, however slight, caused by the suspect, as well as how and why any injuries to the suspect occurred.

You will be judged according to the totality of the facts and circumstances known to you at the time. The essence of context is simply this: anything you want the jury to consider in your defense should be provided at all stages of your post-incident reporting and testimony. While the Plaintiff's attorney has his own reasons for taking your deposition testimony, your reason is simple: this is likely the first time you have had the opportunity to fully explain all of the factors you relied upon in making your decisions and responding to the threat or resistance of the suspect.

> *The essence of "context" is simply this: anything you want the jury to consider in your defense should be provided at all stages of your post-incident reporting and testimony.*

Every question you will be asked has a purpose: it lays a foundation. That foundation is to either set up the Plaintiff's theory of your misconduct, or it is to prove the fact of your misconduct. If there is any opportunity to take your testimony out of context in order to support their contentions, it will be exploited. Your job is to maintain an acute awareness of the underlying intent and meaning of each question put to you. Make sure you keep context in the foreground of your answers.

Relax...Just a Little

At this point in the timeline, many officers get worked up about the whole process, feeling anxious about the unknown as well as being accused of misconduct. It is normal to feel a bit intimidated by the prospect of being a defendant in civil court. Some let their imaginations get so far ahead of their ability to keep up that they actually end up freezing, damaging their testimony in both deposition and in court.

It is time to relax, just a little. Having a realistic perspective about this process is important:

- **Plaintiffs' attorneys are not god-like.** They are people who are doing a job. They don't know everything there is to know about the case because you haven't comprehensively told them your side of the facts. They have only read your report(s) and maybe your interview(s). They also have a perspective on the case that you don't share. They either believe you are a thug or an incompetent based on the story their client gave them. They likely believe that officers routinely lie. Some are just in it for the money the case represents (it is their J-O-B, after all).

  Each and every one of them is beatable if:

  o You reacted reasonably to the Plaintiff's behavior and within the "reasonable officer standard"; and,

  o Your reporting of your perception(s) immediately following the event was sufficient in providing the facts known to you at the time so that others who were not on-scene at the time can understand what you knew and saw; and,

  o Your documentation of the evidence was sufficient to prove the facts of the event, which, in turn, should assist in proving your proper conduct; and,

  o You are prepared to enter the world of confrontation fought with words, arcane rules, and limitations to evidence your defense will be permitted to provide to the jury. You may not agree that all of these limitations are fair, but you will, nonetheless, be required to abide by the confines of this process.

- **Knowing how they are going to attack you permits you to prepare a defense.** If you knew that John "The Hammer" Smith, a recently retired professional heavyweight fighter was going to walk up to you at 12:00 noon tomorrow and, with his right hand, punch you with malice aforethought in the nose before he took you to the ground and pounded you into meat, should you be alarmed? I would suggest that "concerned" might be a better fit than "alarmed." Forewarned with this information, you will likely have three or four other officers standing around you, dressed like you, armed like you, and willing to help defend you when The Hammer strolls up to you. It will likely not turn out as it might have if you did not have this information prior to your meeting with John. You need to tactically prepare for your deposition with the same intensity as you would to deal with The Hammer.

The step-by-step approach suggested in this book will help you prepare to defend yourself in the deposition, and, in turn, your court testimony. It will take some effort. While this process of defending yourself is simple, it is not necessarily easy. Knowing how the Plaintiff's attorney will attack you gives you an edge. Being forewarned of the likely points of attack provides you with the ability to prepare while decreasing the likelihood of being caught off guard. But it will require you to make the effort to articulate the reasonableness of your actions and beliefs with sufficient clarity that each juror will understand and identify with. Intense preparation is the only way that is going to predictably happen.

- **You are in the "going-to-court business."** As an officer, you are essentially a criminal investigator as well as a prosecutorial witness. You investigate reports of crimes, collect evidence, apprehend criminal offenders, and then testify in order to provide the jury with the facts of your investigation. Going to court is what you do. Your participation in this civil case is simply "going to court" in a different context, but it is still a courtroom with a judge, bailiff, clerk, jury, litigators, and audience members. You will be doing what you always do—explaining your observations and decisions. The only real difference is that of your role as the defendant.

Last, but not least...

The burden of proof in a civil trial is different than that of criminal trial. In a civil trial, a plaintiff must prove that it was more likely than not or a "preponderance of the evidence" that you are guilty of the allegations. This is a much easier standard of proof to meet than the more familiar criminal standard of "beyond a reasonable doubt." So your function has not changed in reality: you will be required to give sworn testimony. In your role as a criminal prosecution witness, you are required to prove your version of the facts. Civil court? No difference. You need to prove "what did you know, when did you know it, and how did you respond to it" to prevail in your case.

Thinking that because you did a good job on the street and handled the incident within policy, law, and training will automatically result in being vindicated by the jury is naïve and a recipe for disaster. Preparation for this event is the key to properly engaging in this confrontation. If you knew you were going to be in a gunfight on your next shift, you might think of spending some range time practicing those skills and tactics you might need to prevail. If you knew exactly how that gunfight was going to transpire, you would be better served in practicing only those specific skills.

Entering into sworn deposition testimony is no different than the need for battle preparation—you want to limit your errors and misjudgments while denying the opposition superior positioning and materiel to use against you.

Entering into sworn deposition testimony is no different than the need for battle preparation—you want to limit your errors and misjudgments while denying the opposition superior positioning and materiel to use against you.

The subsequent chapters will assist you in meeting the challenge of providing a deposition that is professional, accurate, and useful in your defense. The focus is upon you. This doesn't change the fact that you are the law enforcement professional in the room, the only one who actually knows what you did and why you did it. You are 100% in charge of your testimony.

If you wish to win this case, prepare yourself to give the best testimony of your life. While it may be too late to rewrite your first report to be as comprehensive as you now wish it had been, or to have been more detailed during your first interview, your preparation from this point forward can make all the difference in the outcome of your case. While your testimony in the criminal trial likely focused on the criminal defendant's actions, *your* actions will be the focus during your upcoming deposition and subsequent civil trial. You must prepare from that perspective.

You did the job on the street. Now do the job that is required to prevail in the civil trial.

Chapter One Summary:

- The deposition you are about to give will set the foundation for the Plaintiff's attorney's strategy in court. It is in your best interest to understand all you can about this process that you are about to enter, and to prepare for it like you have never prepared for testimony before.

- The world of testifying in civil litigation is different from your customary experience in criminal or traffic court. Understanding the context of your role as a civil defendant assists you in shifting gears and focusing upon the requirements of preparing for your deposition and later trial testimony.

- While plaintiffs' attorneys are not god-like and most are simply average attorneys, you are operating in their environment. The opposing attorney may be working for a large portion of the monetary judgment his client might receive. Or he may also be working for court awarded attorney's fees if he prevails. In either case, he's motivated to be thoroughly prepared and capable in his conduct of the trial and his examination of you.

- It is through your thorough and comprehensive preparation that you will have the best chance of providing accurate and complete testimony.

Deposition Preparation:
Know the Plaintiff's Theory

Know the Allegations Against You

In order to know what to prepare for, you will need to familiarize yourself with the allegations against you. This is contained in the document, "Complaint for Damages and Demand for Jury Trial." In the Complaint and Demand, the Plaintiff lays out his theory of the case. There will be several sections:

- **Introduction.** This is a paragraph generally describing the lawsuit ("…a civil rights action seeking compensatory and punitive damages from defendants for violating various civil rights under the United States Constitution…").

- **Jurisdiction and Venue.** This section describes the sections of the US Code as well as the Amendments to the Constitution the Plaintiff is alleging you to have violated. It will also describe why that particular court has jurisdiction over this case.

- **Parties.** This gives the name of the Plaintiff(s) and his relationship to the lawsuit. Also listed are the names of the known defendant officers, supervisors, command officers and chief of police or sheriff, as well as the city, county or state being sued. Also named will be "Police Officer Does 1-

10 (or more)," permitting them to name other officers who are later discovered.

- o **Your spouse may also be named as a party.** In those "community property" states where each spouse has a claim to the other's income and property holdings, the spouse of each defendant officer will be named in the lawsuit in the event the officer is held personally liable for the Plaintiff's losses.[4]

- **Facts Common to All Claims for Relief.** This will be a vague, general outline of the facts the Plaintiff will later offer. You may or may not recognize many of the "facts" or events they allege to have as occurred and they might read like the following:

  - o On or about (the date of the incident), at or near 1234 Main Street in Anywhere, USA, Defendant JONES, who was on duty as an Anywhere City Police Officer, detained and arrested decedent for no reason and without probable cause or reasonable suspicion.

  - o JONES fired his handgun at the decedent, striking decedent and causing him to experience pain and suffering, emotional distress, and mental anguish. The decedent died as a result of multiple gunshot wounds suffered at the hands of JONES.

  - o On information and belief, at the time of the shooting, a reasonable officer in the position of JONES would not believe that decedent was armed or posed an immediate threat of death or serious physical injury to anyone, or had committed any crime. Further, decedent was not resisting arrest or attempting to flee, and there were several alternative means of responding to the situation without using deadly force.

Assuming none of this is true, you will either laugh or cry, or more likely, become angry that anyone would accuse you of such outrageous behavior. Get angry if it works for you, but

---

[4] It is always beneficial to forewarn your spouse that if you are sued, your spouse will also be named. Spouses are like bosses…unpleasant surprises are never good.

understand this: the outrageous accusations have barely begun. You will be accused of depriving loved ones of their "life-long love, comfort, support, companionship, society, care, and sustenance of the decedent…" "The decedent had turned his life of gangs, drugs, alcohol, violence, and crime around, was beginning school and had committed to pay both rent to his parents and child-support to the mothers of his children…" If the Plaintiff was the person you originally arrested and/or forced you to respond with force, there might be other claims of his not being able to live a normal life, inability to sleep due to nightmares, breaking out in a cold sweat from fear at the sight of a police car following him, etc., because the arrest and abuse at your hands "was willful, wanton, malicious and done with an evil motive and intent, and with a reckless disregard for the Plaintiff's rights and safety."

At this point, you know the Plaintiff's preliminary story and how it likely differs greatly from your present memory and the facts included in your report. Be assured that while the Plaintiff's version of the fact pattern often changes as the case progresses, this is a good place to begin your preparations.

Specific Allegations of Misconduct

What will be of greater use to you in your preparations is the "Claims for Relief" section within the "Claims and Demand." Typically you will see a claim for each alleged violation:

- **Unreasonable Search and Seizure—Detention and Arrest (42 U.S.C. §1983) Against Defendant JONES.** This tells you that they will be attacking your initial detention and arrest of the suspect/plaintiff. Your preparations should include:

  o The factors leading you to believe you had sufficient reasonable suspicion to detain and sufficient probable cause to arrest the Plaintiff. If it was a consensual contact, what were the circumstances leading a person to believe he was free to disregard the presence of an officer.

○ Reviewing and relearning the basics of arrest. You need to become fluent in the definitions of "reasonable suspicion," "probable cause," when a seizure takes place, and what constitutes an arrest. If you are going up against an opposing attorney who has taken classes in "police misconduct litigation," you will likely be asked about your training in basic police law covering search and seizure of persons and force law (both statutory and case law). Be sure to obtain the actual lesson plans, handouts, and/or PowerPoint presentations from your academy and in-service trainers to assist in your review.

- **Unreasonable Search and Seizure and Due Process— Excessive Force and Denial of Medical Care (42 U.S.C. §1983) Against Defendants JONES and DOE OFFICERS.** You are being accused of excessive force against the Plaintiff.

  ○ Your homework is to ensure that you are able to articulate and justify the "totality of the facts and circumstances known to you at the time" of your force response. This includes from the first time you initiated the physical arrest through transporting the Plaintiff to the jail facility where the prisoner was handed off to corrections personnel.

  ○ Additionally, be prepared to explain how you provided medical aid to the Plaintiff. This includes the first-aid you provided, any aid provided by medical personnel in the field, and/or how you ensured there was transportation to a hospital (e.g., you requested an ambulance be dispatched). Expect to discuss any delays in providing medical attention caused by your reasonable tactical concerns at the time.

- **Substantive Due Process (42 U.S.C. §1983) Against Defendants JONES and DOE OFFICERS.** The Plaintiff's attorney will attempt to convince the jury that your actions were so outrageous and beyond normal expectations that they "shocked the conscience," constituted a "reckless disregard for," and that you were "deliberately indifferent" to the Plaintiff's civil rights.

- ○ Your preparations will include explaining why, based on your perception of the suspect's threat, resistance, or both, your force response was objectively reasonable, proportionate, within the standards of the training you have received, as well as something any reasonable officer might be expected to do.

- **Municipal and Supervisory Liability (42 U.S.C. §1983) Against Defendants CITY, JONES, and DOE SUPERVISORS.** Plaintiffs are alleging that the city, your administration, supervisory staff, and officers had a custom, policy and practice of:

  - ○ Employing and retaining officers who were abusive and known to use excessive force;

  - ○ Inadequately supervising, training, controlling, assigning, and disciplining officers;

  - ○ Maintaining grossly inadequate procedures for reporting, supervising, investigating, reviewing, disciplining, and controlling intentional misconduct.

  - ○ Failed in their duties to encourage citizen complaints, and made the reporting of citizen's complaints difficult or even impossible for the average person to make. These allegations may also include that the agency, supervisor, or desk officer/personnel attempted to intimidate or discourage the Plaintiff and his family from complaining about the officer's intentional misdeeds.

  - ○ Having and maintaining an unconstitutional policy, custom, or practice of detaining subjects without reasonable suspicion, arresting individuals without probable cause, using excessive force, including deadly force, failing to obtain medical care, and depriving persons of life, liberty, and property so as to shock the conscience of society and the courts, these acts were done with a deliberate indifference to the rights and safety of individuals.

  - ○ Your preparation will consist of ensuring that you can explain how your agency investigates misconduct, and how discipline for policy infractions and violations is handled.

o   You will also want to be able to explain your knowledge and experience of how supervisors take corrective action in your agency, as well the reporting procedures for citizen complaints.

There may be other claims included in the Complaint. Each will provide a general understanding of the areas in which you may have to defend your actions. You will not be certain exactly what the Plaintiff's case will be until the judge has made rulings and determined what will and will not be permitted at trial, as well as which individual(s) and entity(ies) (e.g., the city, county, or state) will be dismissed from the suit.

The Complaint will conclude with a "Prayer for Relief" asking for damages to be determined at trial, as well as a demand for either a bench trial (by a judge only) or a jury trial.

Important Perspective

Now is the time to understand that this process is something you signed on for when you took your oath, accepted your badge, and stepped on to the streets. Take a deep breath and remember that you are a volunteer, not a victim. As an officer, you chose to be a public servant in a warrior profession. A victim mentality is unhealthy and not useful to anyone with a badge, and it serves no purpose in this extension of your duties.

This is the system. In our free society, it is imperative that our police officers are accountable for their actions. The system inherently requires you to articulate your actions, decisions, and behavior in every instance where the free exercise of movement is prevented by the police—especially when force is employed in that detention or arrest. The system was purposely designed within the Constitution to restrain the government and its agents (read, "you," the police officer) from unreasonably interfering with the freedom of any individual without probable cause or a warrant.

The Purposes/Importance of Your Reports

While the written police report is said to serve multiple purposes, the most important ones in preparing for your deposition are:

1. To justify the arrest of the subject in order to prosecute the offender. Your reports are required to justify your conduct in briefly limiting his freedom of movement, or taking it away altogether through an arrest.

2. You may have also injured or even killed that individual during the course of the arrest. Your reports are written (or interviews given) just as much to protect yourself in the process as it is to prosecute the perpetrator. You must justify your reasonable actions in injuring that suspect based on your reasonable perception of his threatening behavior,[5] or his flight where you had probable cause to believe, based on his extremely violent behavior, that he could not be permitted to escape.[6]

If you are the typical defendant officer, you will see and later hear the Plaintiff tell a much different tale than the facts you remember. You will, typically, believe the Plaintiff is lying. Again, that is nothing new in your world. It is common for subjects to lie to you—sometimes for no reason other than they are talking to a cop. People fabricating a story is natural in your working environment. Your job on the street is to work your way through the lies you are told. This is just a different environment where you again work through the lies that are offered as fact. Big deal. Don't get frustrated. Be workmanlike and prepare.

Your job on the street is to work your way through the lies you are told. This is just a different environment where you again work through the lies that are offered as fact. Big deal. Don't get frustrated. Be workmanlike and prepare.

---

[5] <u>Scott v. Harris</u>, 127 S.Ct. 1769 (2007).
[6] <u>Tennessee v. Garner</u>, 105 S.Ct. 1694 (1985).

Your job is to tell the truth as close to your memory of the event as you can. If you did your job reasonably, spent some effort documenting the suspect's actions and behavior, and your response, *and then* ensured you gathered the physical evidence and witness statements, the facts will then speak for themselves. Let others spin tall tales only to have it crash down around them when compared to the evidence and the rest of the testimony. Just work your way through the system and continue to provide your best possible testimony.

Attend the Depositions of Other Involved Parties

If you are fortunate, others involved in the case will be deposed by the opposing counsel prior to your designated date or time. While you will not likely have the luxury of being able to read these depositions, as the defendant in the case you have the right to sit in any of the case proceedings. That means that as your fellow defendant officers are having their depositions taken you should be there, taking advantage of the valuable intelligence revealed by the opposing attorney's conduct and questioning, including:

- **Case strategy.** The case strategy gets laid out very plainly in the deposition. The questions asked will show that the attorney is attempting to prove that there was no valid "core transaction" (you lacked reasonable suspicion or probable cause when you contacted the Plaintiff or entered the premises); your force was excessive based on the facts that you knew at the time; that the Plaintiff had the weapon but didn't pose an imminent threat—or didn't have a weapon; the Plaintiff was not resisting, etc. Pay attention to the *themes* of the questioning: it provides you with the direction of the Plaintiff's case.

- **Types of questions.** Hearing many of the questions that you will likely be asked is a great advantage. You will be able to identify what subjects you need to research, e.g., agency policy or elements of the relevant criminal codes you believed the suspect violated. Also, you will be able to mentally rehearse your answers to provide the clearest testimony possible.

- **The method and conduct of the opposing attorney.** It's nice to know what to expect. Is he taking the cold-nasty-insinuating approach? Or, is he employing the arrogant-bully method. The calm-clinical-professional approach? The slightly befuddled until he isn't approach? The nice-lady-until-she-guts-you-without-mercy approach? Whatever the opposing counsel's style, a preview is nice to have.

Directly ask your attorney to contact your agency and have you released from the work schedule in order to meet with the attorney and attend each of the depositions. This should also include the depositions of the Plaintiff(s), family members, and any witnesses to the event. Some officers also sit in on the expert witnesses' depositions—especially the Plaintiff's expert. This will permit you to assist your attorney in challenging the expert's opinions.

Your job is to become a student of the case and understand the strategies and tactics the opposing counsel will be using to attempt to convince the jury that his client's story is true.

Your job is to become a student of the case and understand the strategies and tactics the opposing counsel will be using to attempt to convince the jury that his client's story is true. The allegations contained in the Complaint will be the starting point in your preparation for your testimony. Once you understand how you will be attacked, you are better able to prepare your defense of your proper conduct and disprove their version of the facts of this case.

Never simply dismiss as unbelievable the outrageous allegations made by the Plaintiff, and you should expect even more as the case progresses. Jurors don't know your job and depend upon the experts to explain the standards of police behavior and training. What you truly believe to be completely fabricated by the opposing expert may very well sound plausible to the jury. Prepare to respond respectfully and answer authoritatively why your conduct was professional, reasonable, and within the expectations of your training, the law, and your agency's policy.

A Word About Plaintiffs' Experts

When preparing for your deposition it is important to understand the Plaintiff's expert's role in the case against you. The expert's theory is generally going to be apparent in the complaint and all successive documents (interrogatories). In cases brought in federal court, expert witnesses are required to write "Rule 26 reports" describing their background, their qualifications, their opinions and the bases for them.[7] While it is rare, it has happened that the expert's written report is forwarded to your attorney prior to your deposition. Sometimes a preliminary opinion has been submitted. If you are so fortunate as to receive either or both, devour and digest that report, and be prepared to refute the outrageous tactical and legal demands that expert would put on you; tactics you know no reasonable officer would ever think about doing.

It is prudent to expect the opposing expert to criticize most or even all of your decision-making during the call. This expert, with his years of experience, rank, and education has, authoritatively and with an air of utter certainty, set the bar of what he claims a reasonable officer is expected to do given his version of the facts of the case. You should realize that his opinion is offered regardless of the fact that such a thing may never have been expected, trained, or even tried by law enforcement.

You would never walk into an oral board without taking time to think through commonly asked questions. While the deposition is not an oral board, your preparation and forethought is necessary to competently navigate through your testimony and defend against the Plaintiff's expert's allegations, however farfetched they might be. The Plaintiff's expert will be telling the jury his beliefs of your incompetency, errors in judgment, and, often, it will be his opinion your conduct constituted "malicious

---

[7] FRSC §26(a)(2)(B).

intent" or "willfully and deliberately violated the Plaintiff's civil rights."

Look at the incident from an outsider's point of view as if you knew nothing about police work and why officers operate in the manner they do. Then prepare your explanations to help that outsider understand your job, from the most basic *why-you-do-what-you-do-as-a-cop*, to understanding what you saw and why you reasonably perceived the suspect's actions or behavior to be a threat.

> *Look at the incident from an outsider's point of view as if you knew nothing about police work and why officers operate in the manner they do.*

Note: The Plaintiff's expert will likely have many more years in law enforcement than you, likely much more education, and almost always more rank. Rightly or wrongly, this frequently legitimizes his opinion in the eyes of jurors. Only by demonstrating your overwhelming job knowledge (and that of your expert's) will counterbalance to these professional witnesses.

Where Plaintiffs' Experts Come From and How they Got Here

Plaintiffs' experts tend to be former police officers. Many of them held very high ranks (chief or deputy chief) and some are from the largest agencies. They tend to specialize in anti-police, pro-plaintiff testimony. They may have PhDs, law degrees, and many have an impressive string of acronyms following their names. Every defendant officer is shocked and disgusted at some level by the testimony provided by these former officers. This is not because these former officers are testifying against currently serving officers; rather, it is because the defendant officer believes the expert is pandering blatantly false testimony to the jury.

Many of these plaintiffs' experts routinely testify that current officers are "out of control" and resort to violence much more quickly than they did back in the 1960s and 1970s when these experts worked the streets for five years before they promoted to lieutenant. Apparently, these decades were the "golden era of policing" where, according to their testimony, officers rarely resorted to force, almost never shot anyone who had a knife or even a gun, and could talk anyone down who was on drugs or experiencing a psychotic break. They also state they didn't overly rely on the "gadgets" officers have now and "actually talked to people" instead of hurting or killing them.

Go figure…that's not my memory of policing prior to the 1980s, but these guys testify to such under oath. Who knew?

Their orientation to force is nearly universally grounded in the now-discredited "continuum of force" whereby they are able to take almost any force incident and claim officers improperly and excessively "escalated" and failed to "deescalate" properly. These continuums are mechanistic attempts to quantify force, concepts specifically forbidden by the US Supreme Court in Scott v. Harris[8] and Graham v. Connor.[9] Yet, in case after case, they claim that officers violated the continuum's "requirements" of force escalation and, most often, de-escalation, and this apparently intentional failure was the proximate cause of the civil rights violation.

Among the theories of misconduct offered by these expert witnesses is that of the officer "creating the conditions leading to force" with insufficient reasonable suspicion to detain or probable cause to arrest. They may opine that the officer intentionally and maliciously harmed the plaintiff because there is no other explanation for the officer's actions, as no reasonable officer could have believed such force was reasonable. A major line of attack on the officer's actions is the allegation by the plaintiff's expert that the officer(s) engaged in gross tactical failures that resulted in the need to use force. Often they will

---

[8] Op. cit.
[9] 109 S.Ct. 1865 (1989).

accuse the defendant of having *caused* the force event by the very nature of their gross dereliction and tactical incompetence.

Plaintiffs' Experts and Their "Cs" (and Sometimes "Ts")

To create this false impression of tactical failures for the jury, these experts may offer testimony that the officer "violated standard tactical training." They then introduce "The Cs," ranging variously from three Cs to six Cs, with sometimes even a "T" thrown in there for good measure. Several experts have testified under oath as to being the originator of this "universal tactical standard." The trouble is, this "tactical standard" is not a standard at all and very few officers have been trained in it. One expert (also claiming to have originated of the "C" theory) propounds his particular viewpoint at police policy conferences, never telling conference attendees that he is almost solely an expert for plaintiffs, and the content of his lecture is wholly plaintiff's theory presented as the leading liability prevention theory.

The beauty of this theory from the plaintiff's standpoint is that no matter what an officer actually did in the field, the Cs (and occasional T) can be used to explain how the officer was incompetent in his tactics.

According to the plaintiffs' experts, proper tactics must consist of *all* of the following:

Containment. PLAINTIFF'S EXPERT: Officers must set up a perimeter in all calls for service. Escape routes must be calculated and interdiction of fleeing suspects prepared for. This containment must be close enough to effectively surround the suspect, but not so close that the suspect's "cushion of safety"[10] is compressed. This is especially true of any armed mentally ill subject confronting the police.

How it is employed against you: *If these officers had only properly contained/contacted the subject, then none of this violence would have been necessary, and the officers would not have had to overreact. These officers were too close and forced the confrontation, or not close enough and could not react quickly enough to prevent the subject's actions. They are so ill-trained that they did not even set up a perimeter* (on a two officer response to a woman with a knife holding her daughter hostage).

REALITY: No matter where you contact or contain the subject, it will be too close and threatening according to the expert. Or it will be too far away and sloppily devised. Regardless of the initial call, and despite a limited number of personnel available for response, failing to set a perimeter is declared to be a gross tactical failure, and a clear indication of the officers' incompetence contributing to the constitutional violation. For example, in a case where the suicidal subject on a check-the-welfare call was located in an upstairs bedroom, the opposing expert stated that officers failed to address all possible points of escape—the contact officer and two backup officers did not station anyone outside the front of the house to prevent the

---

[10] The concept of the "cushion of safety" is a Plaintiff's theory resulting from training regarding calls for service involving the mentally ill. Officers are legitimately trained "to avoid unnecessarily crowding the mentally ill subject." The mentally ill subject is already in distress (which is why he is being contacted by the police). Fear and confusion due to the disruption of coherent thought is the norm for a subject experiencing a psychotic break, and officers are trained that being too close and crowding the subject may cause the individual to lash out in a defensive reaction.

This is translated by the Plaintiff's expert to mean any action taken by the police to restrict the movement of the mentally ill subject, or any position taken by the contact-officer in communicating with the subject, and is just one of the causative factors of this police-caused force event which violated the subject's rights. The cushion-of- safety theory is a perfect mechanism for criticizing police conduct because the necessary distance for a sufficient "cushion" is ill defined, making any distance the officer chooses to be a "serious" error. Any attempt to set up a perimeter on an armed subject (e.g., knife) to prevent his moving toward uninvolved civilians will be a violation of the "cushion of safety" because it is always too close, regardless of the distance between the officer(s) and the subject.

subject from escaping out of the upstairs bedroom window. This even though there was no attempt by the suspect to escape through the window and the window was never a factor in the case. In another instance, three officers responded to a call of a woman on methamphetamine, armed with knives, holding her family hostage, and were criticized by the expert because one of the officers did not take up a position at the back yard while the other two confronted the suspect at the open front door. In this instance, the officers were not concerned about this woman escaping the house. They were working to prevent her from murdering her family members. While many calls require some type of containment strategy, all police contacts do not require a formal perimeter.

Control. PLAINTIFF'S EXPERT: The officer(s) failed to "control" the subject and caused this shooting or need for force. If the officer(s) had only responded properly, had used the proper tone of voice and words, had not shown their weapons (or had shown their weapons sooner, or later), had not been so disrespectful, had given him less (or more space), allowed him to vent (or not allowed him to be emotionally out of control for so long), not allowed him to move toward them (or attempt to leave the area), then the force would not have been required. Officers, because of this failure, overreacted (or didn't react early enough to prevent violence from occurring) and violated the deceased's/plaintiff's rights.

How it is employed against you: *The fact that these officers used violence against the subject is proof that these officers failed to take adequate, nationally recognized measures to prevent the need for this violence. The officers failed to effectively control the subject (or were obsessed with control or overly controlling), causing the subject to react violently as any normal person would.*

REALITY: Despite what you were taught in your academy classes and defensive tactics courses, you realized after just a few short months on the street that you and other officers cannot "control" anyone without effective reasonable force—or a lot of bodies on top of him. Without some degree of force, all you can do is request, cajole, or threaten the subject to gain his compliance. Absent this ability to reason with the suspect because the suspect is armed and/or physically threatening given the circumstances, no amount of talking, cajoling, or threats can *control* anyone without that person's cooperation. A dialogue must go both ways, and a non-responsive subject cannot be reasoned with. A subject armed with a deadly weapon and intending to employ it cannot be controlled without some type of force. Control is something that is ceded to the officer by the suspect.[11] Without the subject's cooperation or sufficient force to coerce compliance and overcome resistance, there is—and can be—no control.

Calm. PLAINTIFF'S EXPERT: The officers are responsible for failing to calm the subject in this situation. The use of sirens and emergency lights, shouted orders—especially if the officer used forceful, disrespectful, or degrading language—and the officers drawing, displaying, or pointing of his various weapons only serves to confuse and frighten the subject, causing him to act or move in a manner the officers mistakenly believed to be threatening. Or, the officers' actions were deliberate because the officers wanted him to move that way so they would have the opportunity to harm him (*"Because there's no other rational explanation for these officer's actions. No other officer would have done something like this."*).

How it is employed against you: *This officer's outrageous and unreasonable threats, shouting, and display of weapons is proof that he was emotionally out of control during this event, and his inability to maintain a calm demeanor was the causative factor leading to the Plaintiff/Decedent's actions. Or, your actions or tactics were unreasonably threatening, and the Plaintiff/Decedent was frightened, causing him to react to the officer's wrongful and intentional acts. It is apparent that you wanted the subject to move in that manner so you could injure or kill him, e.g., "The officer, suspecting him to have a handgun or knife, told Mr. Smith to take his hands out of his pockets.*

---

[11] The phrase, "Control is something the suspect cedes to the officer," was coined by Thomas V. Benge, Sergeant of Police (retired).

When Mr. Smith pulled a gun out of his pocket, complying with this officer's orders, the officer shot him without first determining whether or not Mr. Smith intended to shoot the officer."

REALITY: There are times that maintaining a calm demeanor and employing "non-threatening communications" can assist subjects who are emotionally out of control (frightened, injured, or in shock), leading them toward a sense of safety and a more rational state of mind. This style of communication can be useful when dealing with the mentally ill who are in crisis and who are capable of responding to oral communications. These calm commands are generally employed where there is little chance of assault and the subject permits the officer the safety to attempt to calm the situation.

However, officers are trained to give clear, forceful commands to subjects in fluid, threatening situations. Those commands are, in every sense of the word, instructions to the individual in how to peacefully resolve this situation without injury. These commands establish the officer's authority (e.g., "Police!") and how not to be injured (e.g., "Get on the ground." "Drop the weapon." "Stop."). Make no mistake: proper police commands properly delivered are an attempt to convince or coerce the individual, conveying with the orders the not-so-subtle threat of violence should the person not comply. While the use of calming language is certainly proper in many situations *if the suspect permits*, other dynamic events involving "tense, uncertain, and rapidly evolving circumstances" likely will not, and often result in a force response through no fault of the officer(s).

Case law requires officers to give a warning prior to responding with force *if feasible*.[12] Feasibility within context is based on your reasonable perception of the time you have to safely issue a command or warning. If the situation is dynamic and rapidly evolving, there may be no time to formulate the command in your mind, shout the warning, have the suspect understand the warning, make a decision to act on that warning or not, and then for you to orient to that compliance or resistance prior to your being harmed. In some cases, it would not be feasible to provide a warning or communicate an order because it was unsafe to do

---

[12] For example, <u>Garner</u>, (1985); <u>Bryan v. McPherson</u>, 590 F.3d 778 (9th Cir. 2009).

so, and shooting, striking, spraying, tasing, or some type of force response is reasonable. However, if you reasonably could have done it, there was time, and your or others' safety would not likely be endangered based on your reasonable perception of the events, then a warning or some type of communication prior to responding with force tools should be made.

Communication. PLAINTIFF'S EXPERT: The officers failed to communicate with each other, and failed to plan their approach, method of contact, and how to safely resolve this incident without defaulting to unnecessary and excessive violence. The officers failed to call for sufficient backup, and failed to call SWAT and negotiators. They did not plan together for the eventual actions taken by this subject. These officers were incompetent in their failure to plan, or their planning was so inadequate as to demonstrate a lack of training and maturity, as well as the deliberate disregard for the rights and safety of the plaintiff.

The officer failed to properly communicate with the subject armed with a knife and experiencing a psychotic break. He should have asked "open-ended questions" giving the subject "an opportunity to reflect, interact, and respond." If the officers had only maintained their own emotional neutrality instead of escalating the threatening atmosphere through their confrontational method that is counter to current training, or, if the officer(s) had only given the proper commands in the expected manner, this subject would not have been injured at all.

How it is employed against you: *The failure to properly communicate between the officers, as well as the lack of critical communication skills demonstrated by this officer in speaking to the subject is plainly proven by the fact that violence against the plaintiff resulted at all.*

REALITY: While there are slowly evolving critical incidents requiring a degree of planning to successfully resolve, most patrol responses rely upon officers resorting to their training and experience in handling a multitude of similar calls over the course of their careers. Training should be thought of—and explained to a jury—as "advance planning" for an event.

Regarding a formal plan, anyone with real world experience knows that a plan is simply a starting point in a list of things that we would like to happen but know probably won't. A plan permits officers to get to a certain point in the situation before having to deviate and improvise due to the changing circumstances they are presently facing.

When presented with a dynamic situation, an officer is also likely to be working with one or more other officers. This may be the hundredth time these officers have responded together to this general pattern of facts and circumstances. Or it might be the first time they've worked together, having met at this call, but their training and individual experiences provide all of the planning necessary to deal with the apparent circumstances. There is no need to "talk things over" prior to responding— except when there is, and that will be determined by each officer at the scene and the type of incident at the time. Their training and expectations based on previous experience is all the planning that is necessary to safely resolve the situation. It is then up to the suspect to permit the officers to enact the "plan."

The expert's assertion that anyone can divert or distract a subject who cannot respond rationally to questions due to apparent psychosis, drug and/or alcohol influence, being in a rage, or in dealing with a subject who is simply choosing not to respond to the officers by simply asking open-ended questions is ludicrous. The plaintiff's expert makes such statements because he knows that very few jurors have ever had to deal with a completely irrational person who was experiencing a mental crisis while posing a danger to themselves or others. Good people on a jury can be susceptible to the idea that, "If you had only talked to her, she would have stopped her threatening actions, but the officer never gave her a chance." The reality, as you know and have personally experienced, is that being unresponsive is just that: the person is not engaging in meaningful dialogue. Asking a paranoid schizophrenic, "What do you think about putting down the knife?" has a zero-chance of making any changes to this unfortunate individual's behavior if he is unable to or won't communicate with you. The suggestion that officers should speak to these individuals employing rational arguments cannot be calculated to assist in concluding this incident without injury to someone.

Confirmation. PLAINTIFF'S EXPERT: Officers are required to "confirm" all dispatched information prior to acting on it. Only through the confirmation of original information can officers make an actual determination of the actions necessary in this call. Officers are irresponsible and reckless without confirming with parents/wife/husband/friends that the individual actually owned a weapon. Without confirming what is actually taking place, officers will violate the subject's rights by making a mistake and employ force for the wrong reasons.

How it is employed against you: *These officers were in such a hurry to resolve this situation that they didn't even take the time to confirm all of the information they were given by Dispatch, and needlessly launched into an orgy of violence against the plaintiff.*

REALITY: Officers regularly operate on incomplete—or even erroneous—information. It is rare that you have, or even could have a complete knowledge of all of the facts concerning all of the players in the incident. No matter how you respond, and no matter what decisions you make, the Plaintiff's expert will decry your lack of confirmation of the facts. It will be because of this so-called lack of diligence, inattention to detail, and incompetence that you needlessly resorted to force with the resulting injuries and constitutional errors.

The fact is, officers are permitted to rely upon "official communications" without question. Officers are not required to confirm information provided by Dispatch or other officers—or apparently informed witnesses who are or can be later identified by the officer—prior to responding with force. Officers are permitted to act upon reasonable though mistaken beliefs based on the totality of the facts known to them at the time, and may base their tactics and force decisions on those circumstances.

Some plaintiffs' experts will assert that officers must also engage in confirmation prior to acting when the information is based upon anonymous information. However, they frequently fail to assert what the state or circuit courts have established in this area. More importantly, they fail to mention that an important factor is whether the anonymous reporting party is reporting a crime in progress versus activity of general criminality.[13]

Command. PLAINTIFF'S EXPERT: The on-scene supervisor did not exercise command authority by directing each officer during the call. He failed to personally speak to each officer and direct them regarding how to implement the "plan" (that was not developed according the standards of "Communication") and what each individual officer's part in this formal strategy might be. The supervisor failed in his duties and did not direct the officers to engage in force, and more importantly, did not tell them to wait for his command before contacting the individual, unnecessarily going hands-on with him, or firing at the plaintiff's son. While the officer may have been a trained Crisis Negotiation Team negotiator, the sergeant should have given direction to the negotiator regarding those negotiations. It is plainly apparent that supervisory command was non-existent in this case, which was a proximate cause of the injuries sustained by the plaintiff.

How it is employed against you: *The supervisor or officer-in-charge (OIC) failed to direct officers into position, and further failed to supervise the officers throughout this incident, passively standing by, therefore intentionally permitting the officers to use force on the subject without justification or reason.*

REALITY: No matter what you do as a supervisor or OIC, your conduct on this call will be declared to be dismal at best and criminal at worst. If you relied upon your experienced and well-trained professionals to self-deploy on, for example, a known-risk (or "felony") traffic stop, you may be criticized for not having *directed* them to their posts. Not only did you fail to "plan" the stop during the pre-stop moments before any contact was made (a *per se* supervisory failure), but you failed to supervise the officers in their actions during the stop.

Police reality is that field supervisors are paid to monitor and assess officer's actions in the field and to intervene when there is

---

[13] "Detentions Based on 911 Calls," *Point of View,* Alameda County District Attorney's Office, Spring, 2005, p. 1, quoting U.S. v. Richardson (7th Cir. 2000) 208 F.3d 626, 630). See also, United States v. Terry-Crespo, 356 F.3d 1170 (9th Cir. 2004), and *United States v. Holloway,* 290 F.3d 1331, 1339 (11th Cir. 2002).

a problem. Because a supervisor or OIC did not directly intervene in the placement of the officers, or tell the officers what to do and how to do it, does not mean the supervisor was neglecting his command authority. One of the purposes of training is to standardize behavior. Officers respond to a set of circumstances in a predictable manner because they are trained to do so. This is reinforced by the experience gained from responding to multiple calls that are similar in nature.

Officers respond to a wide variety of incidents. They can, however, be classified into just a few categories of calls where the officers may successfully apply tactical principles. There are an infinite number of details and circumstances requiring an officer to make considered judgments about how to specifically respond to the particular situation confronting him. If any direction is needed, most officers require little more than general adjustments by their on-scene supervisor. There is no need during a response to a call for service for a supervisor to take each officer by the hand and explain their actions and purpose. Instead, supervisors rely on their officers to take immediate charge of scenes and to contact individuals in a tactically sound manner. If the situation extends and requires a more in-depth response, the supervisor might step in to assist his officers.

Time. PLAINTIFF'S EXPERT: The officers either attempted to contact or go hands-on with the subject too hastily (or were far too delayed) in acting.

These officers created the confrontation by acting too aggressively and by not slowing down the timing of the event (or they were too slow). Time is always on the officers' side. In order to take advantage of time, the officers should have redeployed farther back (or closer) to prevent the need for force. They could leave the scene or, at the very least, moved far enough back so that the subject was not *pressured* by their presence, giving him time to calm down. This would have provided the officers an opportunity to find some option other than force. They could have taken that time to devise a strategy that would lead to mutual cooperation and a peaceful conclusion without the unnecessary force we see in the present case.

How it is employed against you: *Every officer understands through experience and is universally trained to know that time is your friend. These officers rushed to a conclusion for reasons only known to themselves and which no reasonable officer could agree (or they took much too long to intervene, giving the suspect the time to plan).*

REALITY: The uncooperative subject drives the time and timing of the event. If the suspect had cooperated, no force or tactics would have been required. The individual's decision to move toward the officer (or a victim)/away from the officer/reach for a weapon/etc., in the manner he did was the suspect's choice, and not the officer's. The officer was attempting to gain cooperation, but the decision was the plaintiff's/deceased's.

In fast-moving, high-stakes events, aggressive action is almost always called for. With 20/20 hindsight it is relatively easy to suggest alternatives to actions, alternatives which may or may not have been successful at the time and cannot be proven to have been any better than the officer(s)'s decision. When an officer is up to his eyeballs in a "tense, uncertain and rapidly evolving" situation with the suspect driving the threat, he is only able to respond according to his training, experience, and within universal human performance limits to that threat. All else is within the province of fortune tellers and plaintiff's experts.

Chapter Two Summary:

- Knowing the allegations will assist you in defending your actions against the case the opposing attorney is attempting to build against you. Read and understand those allegations in the Complaint. While the focus (and often, the facts alleged) will be refined and changed by the time of trial, this will give you a good basis for beginning your preparations.

- Attending the depositions of other involved parties provides you with intelligence regarding how the Plaintiff's attorney operates.

- The Plaintiff's expert will very likely be a former police officer, and perhaps even a very highly ranked and tenured officer. You will likely be dismayed at this person's testimony and then left speechless at their often fabricated claims as to how officers are "normally" expected to handle an event of this type. Be prepared to explain how and why your actions, decisions, and behavior were typical of officers you work with, and why they were trained and reasonable responses.

CHAPTER THREE

Deposition Preparation

Know Your Fundamentals: Policy, Law, and Training Standards

One of the primary goals of the Plaintiff's attorney is to make you appear incompetent and ill-trained (or even untrained). Because of that, he may attempt to quiz you on your academic knowledge of the fundamentals of policing and specific job knowledge. Jurors are very likely to interpret any lack of fluency in these basics as fecklessness and, worse, being unequal to the task. While one does not equal the other in practice, the world of law and courtrooms revolve around words and their precise meaning, as well as being articulate. Failing to confidently articulate what others might consider to be fundamental core knowledge of your profession will taint their opinion of your actions and decision-making in the case, and may fundamentally affect their verdicts.

As Commander Gordon Graham (California Highway Patrol, retired) teaches, "Things that go wrong in life are highly predictable, and if predictable, they are preventable." The "plaintiffs' playbook" is clear and easy to understand: "If you cannot attack the facts of the case, attack the person involved in the case." Because of this, the following cannot be understated: If you know how your attacker will engage you, whether in the street or in court, it is easy to build a defense against that assault. All you have to do is make the effort.

The "plaintiffs' playbook" is clear and easy to understand: "If you cannot attack the facts of the case, attack the person involved in the case."

You gain an unintended benefit through this preparation: your knowledge of law and policy will deepen, increasing your ability to make reasonable split-second decisions. Concomitant with a better academic grasp of your core professional knowledge is a greater ability to articulate your perceptions and the justifications for your force responses. This translates into greater protection against civil liability as well as heightened professionalism and career security.

Agency Policy

Read, understand, and know the policy(ies) that are involved in this case. Your primary policy review and study will be those policies applicable to your immediate fact pattern. As part of the discovery process, the Plaintiff will demand certain policy sections for his case preparation. Ask your attorney to provide you a list of those policies. Then study those policies until you know them authoritatively.

"Conversational familiarity" means just that: being able to discuss what your policy permits and/or prohibits without the need to refer to your policy. While quoting the whole policy verbatim is not expected, there are going to be some sections you will want to be able to substantially summarize.

Part of the plaintiffs' attorneys' playbook (and a tactic they learn in their continuing legal education courses as required by their state bar associations to maintain their licenses) is to immediately hit you with questions about your policy at the beginning of your deposition. Following the introductions and admonishments about the conduct of the deposition, it will look something like this if they've attended the classes:

ATTORNEY: State your name and spell it for the record?

OFFICER: James Maurice Jones. J-O-N-E-S.

ATTORNEY: Are you currently employed?

OFFICER: Yes, sir.

ATTORNEY: How are you employed?

OFFICER: I'm a police officer for the City of Anywhere Police Department.

ATTORNEY: Do you consider yourself to be a well-trained City / County / State / Federal officer / deputy / trooper / agent?

OFFICER: Yes, sir.

ATTORNEY: Were you trained in your agency policy regarding reasonable force/deadly force/pursuit/search and seizure?

OFFICER: Yes, sir.

ATTORNEY: I would like to explore this topic with you. What does your agency policy…(blah, blah, blah)?

OFFICER: May I refer to my policy?

ATTORNEY: Well, let me ask you this. Were you reading it when you were beating my client?

OFFICER: I did not beat your client. And I was not reading it as I was responding with force to the threat of your client, Mr. Smith, based on his statements, behavior, and assaultive actions.

ATTORNEY: Then you may not refer to your policy. I want to know what knowledge you had about the policy at the time of the incident. That policy was in place to protect my client from excessive force and the deliberate abuse he suffered at your hands. You do believe, do you not, that knowing your force policy is very important to your achieving proper conduct as an officer? Isn't that correct?

This line of questioning *can* take up to an hour—solely focusing on your specific knowledge of the relevant policy, whether it be force, deadly force, pursuit, or search and seizure. The attorney will likely ask you non-sequential questions about your policy, attempting to confuse you about the context of the question. Knowing your agency's policy language will be critical to your defense in this environment.

The better you know your policy, the more quickly the opposing attorney will abandon this line of questioning.

The better you know your policy, the more quickly the opposing attorney will abandon this line of questioning. Like a good military commander, attorneys only exploit success, and they measure their success against your ability to articulate your observations and actions during the event in question. If you stop him cold with informed answers, the attorney will quickly move on in search of better hunting.

Once you have studied and are able to accurately and confidently restate your policy, your preparation should include discussing how your actions applied to and comported with the policy. The Plaintiff's attorney will attempt to convince to the jury the idea that any policy violations you allegedly committed automatically means that all of your decisions were tainted. If you are being sued in state court, allegations of negligence will be a key component of the Plaintiff's main case. While negligence and policy violations should not be a consideration in the reasonableness of your force response in federal court cases, they often have an effect on the jury's perception of your actions. Therefore, it is your job as a defendant to explain how your actions met standards as outlined by your agency's policy manual.

Core Transactions During the Contact

Some lawyers will attempt to ambush you by using legal jargon that is not commonly known to officers in order to make it appear you are untrained and/or incompetent (and therefore ill-equipped to have reasonably performed your duties in this case). One favorite plaintiffs' attorney tactic is to ask whether you believe you had a "valid core transaction." Simply translated, he is asking you, "Do you believe your initial contact of this subject was justified and reasonable?" He may ask, "What was your core transaction with the decedent?" The attorney is asking you to explain how the incident arose and in what basis you contacted his client:

- A consensual contact (also known as a "social contact" in some states) where the subject voluntarily spoke to you in an environment where he was free to disregard the presence of the police.[14]

- Reasonable suspicion which justified a detention. This may have been an investigative or *Terry*[15] stop where you observed unusual or suspicious behavior related to a crime that has occurred, is occurring, or may occur involving the person to be detained. It may have also been a *Terry* frisk for weapons where, following a lawful detention, you performed a cursory search (or pat-down, frisk, etc.) for weapons based on articulable belief that subject was armed or dangerous. That justification may have included both an investigative detention and an officer safety detention, all three (investigative detention, a cursory search for weapons, and/or for officer safety), or simply an officer safety detention (permitted when you can articulate the need to be in proximity to the subject to be detained, and the circumstances indicated there was some threat to your safety, and the circumstances of that detention balanced with the apparent threat of the subject to your safety).

---

[14] Florida v. Bostick, 501 U.S. 429 (1991).
[15] Terry v. Ohio, 392 U.S. 1 (1968).

- Probable cause for an arrest (facts and circumstances leading you to believe the individual had violated the specific elements enumerated in your criminal codes and committed a crime).

The evaluation of your force response, as well as any police action you took (warrant service, traffic stop, pedestrian stop, etc.) will at some point focus upon whether or not there was a legally justified basis for contact. It is a fact-specific, fact-dependent analysis of why you believed you were legally permitted to limit the freedom of the individual in question. If this is a case involving any type of force response, then the legality of your initial contact and subsequent actions may well determine the reasonableness of your force decisions.

For example, the suspect was drawing a handgun from his waistband and got off a shot that struck your ballistic vest before you were able to fire and incapacitate him. It would seem apparent that this is a completely justified shooting. However, if you add the additional fact that you were inside his house without a warrant, without exigence, and only with the consent of an obvious minor who let you in the house because you asked to talk to "daddy," your legal right to be in contact with this individual may be in question and may lead to the loss of your right to legally justified self-defense.[16]

Any force you employed, even in self-defense, may be rendered unjustified and therefore excessive if you had no right to contact the individual in the manner you did, or you cannot articulate the justification for the contact. Your seemingly justified force response *may* be invalidated if:

---

[16] Various federal circuits have a different interpretation of how the events leading up to a force response affect the actual force response, or components of force. For instance, in some circuits, constitutional violations of search and seizure laws and the self-defense shooting of the plaintiff are separate issues to be considered, while in other circuits the initial constitutional violation renders the subsequent force response unconstitutional, even though the shooting was clearly in self-defense. It is your responsibility to know what the limitations are in your jurisdiction.

- You told him to stop—and he complied—without reasonable suspicion.

- You detained him in such a manner that it turned into a de facto arrest without probable cause.

- You arrested the subject without articulating sufficient probable cause.

Your fundamental ability to justify contacting the subject—your constitutionally valid core transaction—must be legally sound and defensible. In exploring this, the Plaintiff's attorney may test your training and expertise by asking:

- "When does a police seizure of a subject take place?"

- "What is required for consensual/social contact?"

- "What is required for a detention?"

- "How were you trained that 'reasonable suspicion' is defined?"

- "What is necessary for an arrest?"

- "How were you trained that 'probable cause' is defined?"

It is incumbent upon you to increase your academic familiarity with the core components of police-subject contacts and have the conversational ability to explain what the legal requirements are when contacting a subject.

Being competent—or even expert—on the street where events must be rapidly responded to when contacting individuals involved in the complex and dynamic events typifying police incidents is essential for attaining proper conduct as an officer. However, that expertise may not be sufficient in assisting you in the legal challenges you face as the defendant in a civil matter against a well-prepared plaintiff's attorney. It is incumbent upon you to increase your academic familiarity with the core components of police-subject contacts and have the conversational ability to explain what the legal requirements are when contacting a subject. You learned them before, once upon a time in the academy. This is simply review in preparation for the battle of words and concepts you are soon to enter. There is no downside to this effort. Your increased level of knowledge will assist you in making sound decisions in your day-to-day work and also help prepare you for testing for promotions and special assignments. This preparation will be a win-win for you, and may spare you a level of pain, discontent, and embarrassment in court.

Force Law

Another likely avenue of attack by opposing counsel is your understanding of the limits and permissions afforded you by federal case law, as well as your state law(s) regarding force. Knowing the law is a professional requirement. However, many officers have trouble articulating key case law language—or even paraphrasing it—when asked. This is a deficit that is often exploited by plaintiffs in civil cases.

At a minimum, you should be conversant with the following cases[17]:

- Scott v. Harris, (2007) 127 S.Ct. 1769.

- Graham v. Connor, (1989) 109 S.Ct. 1865.

- Tennessee v. Garner (1985) 105 S.Ct. 1694, if you shot someone who was fleeing.

- The main force and seizure cases of your federal circuit.

These general cases controlling your conduct and behavior will be held up against your actions when your force response is evaluated. If your federal circuit courts have cases where force laws are modified (e.g., there is no requirement to consider lesser

---

[17] As of this writing, these are the major controlling cases in federal case law involving the guidelines and evaluation of the police force response. Be sure to consult with your local legal authority to ensure you are current with all legal and case law requirements.

alternatives of force; officers are not required to retreat; etc.), know their requirements as well.

While no one expects you to be an attorney, you are a *law* enforcement officer. As such, your familiarity and comfort with the laws you enforce and especially those permitting you to injure and possibly kill another should be, again, conversational.

- If your case involves shooting someone in a standup gunfight, you may be asked the question, "When are you legally permitted to shoot a person?" Your answer should instantly be, "I may respond with deadly force when I have an objective and reasonable belief that my life, or that of another's, is in actual or imminent danger of death or serious bodily injury, based on the totality of the facts known to me at the time. In <u>Scott</u>, the US Supreme Court stated that deadly force must be in response to 'an extreme threat to human life.'" Committing this phrase to memory is just the beginning. Each phrase within this statement may require a comprehensive explanation.

- If you shot someone you mistakenly thought was armed, your explanation will include the fact that you were trained that you may act upon a reasonable belief of threat even if it is later discovered to have been mistaken. Because of human factors limitations (the realities of reaction-response times, where waiting to verify the object is actually a weapon would lead to the officer being fired upon without being able to interrupt that assault), officers are permitted to act upon a reasonable belief of imminent threat to life.

- When challenged, you are comfortable discussing why you are not required to fire one or two rounds, evaluate the status of the threat, and then, if needed, fire one or two more. You are able to discuss the legally required fear of serious physical injury or death, and that you are permitted by training and the law to continue to respond with deadly force and fire into the suspect until you perceive the imminent deadly threat is resolved.

- If asked why you may respond with force that is more injurious than that which the suspect employed, you should be able to explain that officers are empowered to overcome the physical resistance or assault by a suspect with force that can reasonably be expected to stop the threat and take him into custody. The <u>Scott</u> case requires officers to balance the likelihood of injury or death to the suspect with the officer's reasonable perception of threat to the officer or others.

- If asked what the definition of excessive force is, you will confidently give them the definition from <u>Black's Law Dictionary</u>: "Force which is not justified given the totality of the facts known at the time."

- You may be tasked with explaining how force by the police is evaluated. In this instance, you might reply, "All force is context-based, and viewed from the point of view of the officer at the time, or the officer's mindset, and must meet the 'reasonable officer standard.'[18] This was defined in training as 'Would another officer with like or similar training and experience, given the same or similar circumstances, respond in the same way or make similar decisions.' It does not require the officer to make the best decision possible, or to act in superhuman ways. The law requires an officer to objectively and reasonably respond with force based on all of the facts and circumstances known to the officer at the time. This is the main consideration in the evaluation of force per <u>Graham</u>."

- When the opposing counsel inquires, "What was your intent when you shot my client's husband in the head?" you will likely testify to something like, "Because of his threatening behavior, believing that my life and safety were in danger, I had to stop him as quickly as possible. I shot him with the intent of saving my life." When asked if you thought that would kill him, answer honestly, "At the moment I pressed the trigger, I believed I had to stop him to save my life. I saw

[18] California Commission On Peace Officer Standards And Training, Basic Course Workbook Series, Student Materials, Learning Domain 20, Use of Force, Version 3.0, Page 17.

the head and pressed the trigger. I didn't have enough time to consider the ramifications of the shot(s)—it was all happening way too fast. Now, post-event, with lots of time to think about it, I know it is likely that shooting a man in the head with a rifle/handgun/shotgun will kill him. But I didn't think about it like that at the time. I just wanted to stop him from hurting or killing me."

- Being asked a question about why you did not immediately begin CPR on a downed suspect, and why you did not attempt to staunch the blood flow from his gunshot wounds, you are able to explain, "I was trained that medical aid to a person injured by an officer is required by law. That assistance, per my training and law, is satisfied by my radioing in notification of 'shots fired' and by my request for medical assistance. As soon as I was assured the suspect could no longer harm me, I made that radio call. The scene, however, was not yet secure, and I had the duty to secure the scene in order for paramedics to safely arrive and begin advanced life-saving efforts. I performed exactly to the standards per my training." If you did attempt to staunch blood flow, explain the delays caused by the need to handcuff him per your training prior to giving him first aid. This required a second officer to arrive in order to do it safely.

These are just a few examples of the issues you should be able to answer. The citing of cases and the explanation of the law expected of a lawyer is absolutely not needed. What is necessary is an understanding and ability to discuss the limits to police force given the situation you were attempting to resolve, and why you are permitted by your training to respond with the force you did.

If there are collateral issues involved in the case, then the conversational familiarity with the laws and your training governing those activities is essential, such as:

- "Why you are permitted to detain and handcuff all subjects within a residence while serving a search warrant?"

- "What are the factors permitting you to conduct a protective sweep of the residence without the consent of the resident?"

- "When are you permitted to pat-search a person for weapons?"

- "What is the basis for an "officer-safety detention?"

- "When are you permitted to handcuff a subject during a detention and when are you not?"

- "What is your responsibility under the (state) vehicle code as an officer during a vehicle pursuit?"

The ability to explain the laws regarding force, pursuits, detentions, arrests, and the constitutional requirements of your public contact is "core job knowledge." Consider what your own response might be to a surgeon who doesn't seem to understand the biological processes of the body or fumbled around trying to remember human anatomy. The chances are that you would not permit him to perform surgery on you or a family member. In the same way, a police officer who cannot speak comfortably about the laws permitting him to use force against and/or arrest someone is often perceived by the juror as ignorant and untrained. The fact that this is not the truth and that you acted within the law becomes immaterial; your inability to articulate this core knowledge is seen as unforgivable ignorance. This is not pretty in front of a jury and will only hurt your case.

Know Your Force Tools

You will likely be closely questioned about your training and knowledge regarding the weapons you carry—especially the weapon or weapons you employed against the Plaintiff or the deceased. Knowing the make, model, caliber, maker of the ammunition, bullet type and weight, the number of rounds you carry in your handgun (the number of rounds in the magazine plus the total number of rounds you carry into the field, etc., will demonstrate a level of expertise and competence to the jury. Sitting in a deposition with every word being taken down is not the first place to consider these questions. Be assured your ignorance of your tools will be introduced to the jury.

One of the biggest problem areas with force tools centers around the technical knowledge of the TASER. Many officers, in fact most, carry it. They have a reasonable understanding of when to employ it and do a good job responding to the specific threat. In a case where the officer hit the suspect with both probes and achieved full lockup, there is no question the defendant officer in the TASER lawsuit knew how to operate it because he hit the suspect. That is why the officer is in the courtroom as a defendant.

In the field, a detailed knowledge of its technical specifications is not necessary to achieve proper conduct—you reasonably responded with the TASER, you hit him in reasonable areas of the body, and the device worked as advertised (or didn't, if that was the case). However, the "surgeon's knowledge problem" arises when an officer is unsure of the tool's specifications. It is worse when he misremembers how the TASER functions or the limitations of deployment and gives wildly incorrect information. This includes:

- Specifics about voltage and amperage.

- The minimum spread necessary for an effective probe-tasing and how far away from the suspect the device must be in order to obtain that minimum probe spread.

- The maximum distance your particular cartridge is designed for.

- Whether or not a person who is wet or standing in water may be tased.

- What constitutes a "height" where a subject may not be tased if not in a deadly force situation.

- If or when an obviously pregnant woman may be tased.

- The data capture capabilities of the TASER.

- How the standard five-second cycle may be extended indefinitely.

- Whether shouting, "TASER! TASER! TASER!" constitutes a warning to the subject that he is about to be tased (it does not).

- Whether or not it is mandatory to always, without exception, provide a warning to the subject prior to tasing (it is not).

- Why it is suggested but not mandatory for a second officer to be on scene to act as a "cover officer" and be armed with a firearm when the TASER is employed.

Each of these questions have been posed to defendant officers. Each of these questions are included in this list because the defendant officers in their depositions failed to accurately respond to one or more of these basic questions about their knowledge of the force tool they employed against the plaintiffs.

Prior to your deposition, research your force tools—OC Spray, TASER, baton, and firearm. Make a formal appointment with your agency's lead instructor for that force tool with the expressed purpose of reviewing the technical specifications, function, and limits to the tool. This review should also include all policy provisions and limitations on its use. Do not assume that because you have carried the weapon for the last ten years and took a "re-cert" class a year and a half ago that you "know" what you need to know. You are about to be tested on your knowledge in detail via open-ended questions. Go into this review with an "innocent mind," as if you were learning about it for the first time. Then consider reviewing this knowledge by "teaching" the instructor. Have him correct any mistaken information you may have. Go over any mistakes again until you have it perfect.

Prior to your deposition, research your force tools—OC Spray, TASER, baton, and firearm.

Knowing the specifications peculiar to that particular tool, the weight, manufacturer, optimal distances, maintenance requirements, nomenclature, etc., affords you the opportunity to demonstrate your expertise and professionalism. Answering every question correctly, with the confidence borne out of certain knowledge will create a disincentive to the Plaintiff's attorney to continue a line of questions that makes you look well trained and knowledgeable—again, anything that puts you into a more professional light is not in the best interest for his case. The result will be fewer questions about your core competencies, and more about the incident, your actions and responses, and your perceptions of the suspect's behavior. This is exactly where you want the inquiry to focus.

Your Training History

Your training history will likely become a topic of inquiry. Prior to your deposition, meet with your training manager to go over your records. Minimally, you will want to know how many hours of training you have received:

- Total in your career.

- Of academy training.

- In the topics specific to this lawsuit.

For example, you are being sued in a domestic disturbance case. The male opened the door, refused to allow you to check the welfare of the female, and suddenly closed and locked the door before you could get a foot in to block it. Hearing a shout and a female scream from inside, you stepped back, drew your weapon, and kicked open the door. You then saw him rushing at the female with a knife raised in his hand, screaming something (witnesses in the next apartment later testified that he was shouting he was going to kill her). You took in the scene instantly: her face contorted in fear, arms outstretched defensively, backing up blindly, husband pulling back the knife to strike as he rushed at her. You shot him in time to stop him, and he was unfortunately killed. Now the female, as executor of his estate, is suing you for the wrongful death of her husband and the father of two of her five children.

In preparation for your deposition, you will want to know the approximate dates of your training courses (month and year is sufficient), the number of hours of each course, as well as the total number of hours you have had in courses addressing minimally the following topics:

- Domestic disturbance and violence calls.

- Exigent circumstances and non-consensual entry into a residence.

- Options when legally checking the welfare is blocked by an individual.

- Any edged weapon training.

- Deadly force policy and/or law.

- Firearms training.

- Scenario-based training or force-on-force training, especially any scenarios related to the incident, including "no-shoot scenarios."

- Limitations in human attentional load.

The Last Word on Preparing for Articulating Your Fundamentals...

Many officers are resistant to making the effort necessary to prepare for their depositions. It's natural for humans to avoid what may seem to be unnecessary extra work, and the hours of meetings and study are certainly unappealing. However, you are going to court. Unless you die or flee to Southwest Asia, you cannot avoid it (by the way, even if you die, the trial will still be held, but will result in your version of the facts being more difficult to present to the jury). And you will be deposed. In that deposition, you have a very good chance of being asked questions about the topics detailed in this chapter.

The length of this inquiry into these topics and core job knowledge will depend solely upon you. Attorneys exploit weakness and avoid strength. If there is blood in the water, you can be assured that there will be a feeding frenzy at your expense.

And if you perform poorly on your core job knowledge in your testimony at deposition, you may be assured that performance will be highlighted in trial before the jury. At trial, it will be too late to rehabilitate your testimony. It doesn't help later in trial to know what you didn't know in deposition. The Plaintiff's attorney will happily suggest that while you may know the answers today in court, you obviously didn't know the information at deposition, and therefore didn't know what you were doing during your interaction with his client.

Take the time to prepare yourself. The best case scenario will be that the opposing attorney has not attended classes on suing the police, is not a police specialist, and will come at you like an attorney who is litigating any other type of case. In this instance, you will not face detailed questioning about your agency policy, job history, and knowledge. The worst case will be the attorney who teaches at the continuing legal education training conferences to attorneys entitled, "How to Win in Police Misconduct Cases," and is a stone cold pro at making defendant officers look stupid in front of juries. Given the two extremes, the attorney you face will likely be somewhere in the middle: a legal professional who is competent and prepared. If you were competent in your actions and decisions in the street, took the time to prepare a reasonably comprehensive first report or gave a functional and competent first interview, and are willing to take the time to ready yourself to meet what is a known threat in both the deposition and later in the courtroom, you are far more likely to be satisfied with your performance at the conclusion of your testimony.

Chapter Three Summary:

- Your fundamental job knowledge will be explored during the deposition, and any lapses in your knowledge will be a point of focus by the opposing attorney later at trial in front of the jury.

- Take the time to learn your agency policies, training materials, current force laws, search and seizure laws, and other laws relevant to your case in depth. This will reinforce your professionalism in the eyes of the jurors. It additionally assists you in articulating your decision-making in your day-to-day contacts with the public.

- During your deposition, the time the Plaintiff's attorney spends exploring your job knowledge will be inversely proportionate to your ability to articulate those standards. The better you articulate your job knowledge, the less time you will be questioned. Like a good military commander, the opposing attorney will exploit your weaknesses and bypass your strengths. Your task is to make your core job knowledge bulletproof, so that the majority of the time you spend testifying is about the incident and your proper conduct in responding to the Plaintiff's criminal behavior.

The Deposition

A Vehicle of "Discovery"

A deposition is a formal component of the discovery process, permitting both parties to discover the testimony, evidence, and strategies of the opposition. It provides the means for both sides to prepare their cases and avoid "trial by ambush." Surprises in court are something each side wishes to avoid. If there is a later attempt to introduce information at trial without first disclosing it to the opposition, it will generally be excluded and not be available to the jury to consider.

While lawyers will declare the deposition is simply a vehicle of gathering information about the present case, in reality, it is an opportunity to discover much more. Previously related cases, your job, education, experience, training, prior employment, etc., are generally open for discussion while you are under oath. While your attorney will likely object, the Plaintiff's attorney is permitted to go down *almost* any rabbit hole in the case until it is completely mined for information. From the officer's point of view, it often feels like a fishing expedition governed by the rules of evidence for the benefit of the Plaintiff and his case. By the way, this is how the Plaintiff will feel when he is giving deposition testimony to your attorney. Such is the nature of depositions.

Every word contained within the resulting deposition transcript will be scrutinized by the Plaintiff's attorney and their highly paid experts for any apparent or actual inconsistencies and omissions by you during any previous criminal court testimony against the Plaintiff, Grand Jury and/or coroner's inquest testimony, your administrative interviews, as well as any written reports you or others made in this case. You will likely be asked the same questions during your civil trial that you were asked in your deposition, with all previous reports and testimony cross-indexed and noted by the opposing attorney. The functional purpose of the deposition from the Plaintiff's perspective is to gather material and information to impeach your later testimony, making it appear to the jury that you are untruthful.[19]

Like you, jurors hate liars. The Plaintiff's attorney will do everything possible to make it appear that you are inconsistent, evasive, and untruthful. If you offer him an opening through sloppy reporting or inconsistencies with any prior testimony—including the deposition—the opposing attorney may be able to seize an advantage he would not have otherwise had. If he is able to make it appear that you have been untruthful, the jury will likely turn on you, resulting in a judgment for the Plaintiff, and a bonanza in attorney's fees for his lawyer. That's exactly why every minute of preparation and attention to detail prior to the deposition—and knowing your case inside and out—is valuable. Preparation pays off in the long run with your comprehensive and consistent testimony.

Depo Logistics

You and your co-defendant officers, if any, will generally be required to travel to the Plaintiff's attorney's office to give your testimony, while the Plaintiff(s) and their witnesses will provide deposition testimony in your attorney's office. Witnesses who are deposed will generally travel to the closest office, or a mutually agreed upon location to give their testimony.

---

[19] "One of the prime reasons to spend the time and money to depose an adverse witness is to gather impeachment material."
http://www.newdorf.com/top_ten_killer_deposition_questions.

Occasionally, the attorneys may agree to conduct the deposition at other locations if more convenient, or even by telephone, although that is rare.

The deposition is generally held in a conference room and is a private proceeding. The only persons who may be present are:

- The plaintiff(s).

- The opposing attorneys and their assistants, if any. There may be multiple plaintiffs' attorneys, as well as multiple defense attorneys (I once sat in a very crowded conference room providing deposition testimony before a total of eleven plaintiffs' attorneys or their assistants, plus the father of the decedent).

- The defendant officer(s).

- A stenographer, or court reporter, taking down the witness' sworn deposition testimony.

Some federal circuit courts permit expert witnesses to attend. While the expert will not be permitted to participate in the actual questioning, he will be assisting the Plaintiff's attorney by analyzing your answers as well as feeding the attorney written questions to ask you. Depending upon the Plaintiff's attorney's level of experience, the expert may also be directing the course of your questioning for the attorney. His presence permits a real-time evaluation and follow-up of your deposition testimony.

A certified videographer may also be present, video-recording your testimony. If, for any reason, you are unable to testify at trial, the video recording may be played for the jury as your sworn testimony. It may also be played in an attempt to impeach your earlier or current testimony during the trial.

NEVER LET THE INFORMAL SETTING FOOL YOU. This is serious business. This is your first opportunity as a civil defendant to be questioned under oath about your actions and behavior. Almost as much as your initial report or interview, this deposition will set the foundation for your entire testimony in this civil court case.

You will be questioned detail by detail as the minutiae of the case is explored and examined. A twenty second fight may take four to six hours—and sometimes more—to explain. Some officers have been forced to provide two or even three days of deposition testimony. You likely have never experienced this depth of exploration before. Pay attention, answer the question, and do not be surprised if you are asked incredibly naïve questions about your job—sometimes the most basic questions seem to be the most difficult to answer.

Hours will pass. You will ask for breaks, perhaps take a lunch break, and may be called back for additional days of deposition depending on the opposing lawyer and complexity of the case. There is no standard limit in how long a deposition might last (although you cannot be deposed for more than eight hours without your permission in most federal circuits). It will end when the attorney conducting the deposition finishes his questions.

At the Depo

The deposition, because it is held in private, permits the Plaintiff's attorney to act in ways that he or she might not dare to in open court. It gives them the opportunity to size you up for the first time, and to gauge the value of this case regarding their time and effort. Some will seek to get you angry, some will attempt to intimidate you. Others will be gracious in a ploy to get you to relax. Some will just be professional—ardent, but professional.

The truth is, lawsuits have been won in deposition because a squared away, competent, and prepared officer was able to convince opposing counsel that there was no money in the case.

The truth is, lawsuits have been won in deposition because a squared away, competent, and prepared officer was able to convince opposing counsel that there was no money in the case. Take away the potential rewards, and this case that was previously about "social justice for this downtrodden victim of police abuse" is suddenly not so urgent and the officer's actions apparently not so outrageous. That attorney then turns his focus to cases that are more likely to provide him with income, which makes sense because this is his job. It doesn't happen often, but it can and has.

You want to be that officer who causes the attorney to question the value of the case. The way to do that is to, first, have done a solid job on the street. Second, it is vital know your job—your policies, the law(s) you were enforcing, as well as a comprehensive knowledge of your case. It is equally important that you conduct yourself confidently yet not arrogantly, be articulate but not helpful, and to demonstrate you have command of your emotions.

Consult with your attorney concerning appropriate attire. Most attorneys ask you to wear a suit and tie, although some suggest "business casual." Others will want you to wear your uniform. Always be early for the deposition, well-dressed, and ready for business.

Conduct and Admonitions

You will enter the conference room, likely accompanied by your attorney. Get your game face on. Now is the time for the opposing counsel to observe a confident, well-prepared professional who is ready to answer any question about his personal and professional life, and to explain his reasoning and actions based on the Plaintiff's behavior and actions. Follow your attorney's directions and lead (which is good advice throughout this entire civil process).

Most plaintiffs' attorneys, but not all, will introduce themselves and shake your hand—it likely won't be a warm handshake. You will be briefly introduced to the court reporter, and will generally be seated next to her. This affords the court reporter the best opportunity to hear your testimony.

Your job is to be businesslike, professional at all times, and courteous no matter how rude or abrasive the opposing attorney is to you. You are being judged not only by your actions and decisions in the field, but by your conduct and bearing in every court proceeding, including this one. Sit down, be still, and speak clearly and confidently. This is your chance to explain why your reasonable perceptions of the Plaintiff's behavior led to your reasonable actions based on your training and experience.

This is your chance to explain why your reasonable perceptions of the Plaintiff's behavior led to your reasonable actions based on your training and experience.

You will be sworn in by the court reporter with the same oath you take in court. As you do in court, sit at attention, look the reporter in the eye, hold your right hand up rigidly, and clearly say, "I do."

You will be asked to state and spell your name. Within a few minutes, generally after he introduces himself for the record, the opposing attorney will typically provide you with admonitions and instructions regarding the conduct of your testimony. You will be asked if you have ever given deposition testimony before. If you have, the attorney may or may not ask if you are familiar with the rules and admonitions concerning deposition testimony.

These admonitions will generally cover the following, although this list is not exhaustive. You will be asked if you agree to or understand each of the following points:

- **Penalty of perjury.** You will be told that the oath you have just taken to tell the truth carries the same penalties for perjury as the oath given in court.

- **Speak one at a time.** In day-to-day conversation, it is common for individuals to anticipate the question and answer well before the individual speaking is finished with the sentence. However, the court reporter is attempting to accurately record every word, and talking over the attorney will result in a confused or an erroneous transcript. Do not anticipate the question. As when testifying in criminal court, wait for the attorney to finish before speaking.

- **Not understanding a question.** You may not understand a question as it is put to you. Ask for it to be repeated and/or for it to be rephrased. If you do not ask for the question to be repeated or clarified, it will be assumed that you understood the question as it was asked.

- **You don't remember.** Human memory changes and fades. Depositions are often two and three years (and possibly more) post-incident. If you don't remember, say so. It is a legitimate and honest answer. You may also review prior testimony in order to clarify your testimony.

Note: it is typical for an officer to not remember a detail, or to remember it differently at this late date than in an interview or report given contemporaneously to the incident. Explain the fact that the incident was long ago, and that your memory of it is not the same as it was when it was fresh. While you don't remember it *now* the way you first reported it, your first report was more accurate than your memory. Again, human memory is fallible.

Some officers get upset and frustrated by this apparent contradiction in their deposition (and later court) testimony when compared to their initial reporting or interview, thinking it appears they are being deceptive. Good advice? Don't worry about it unless you are actually being deceptive. If you now remember that something was "red," but in your interview, hours or days after the incident you said the color was "blue," that would be honest and in compliance with your oath. You may also have been mistaken in your original reporting, but later learned the facts were different than you understood them at the time. Because your memories are either inaccurate now or were when you first reported your perception of the facts *does not* mean you are being untruthful in your testimony. It means you are human and told the truth in each instance.

- **Give verbal answers.** Proper answers are "Yes," and, "No," rather than "uh-huh" and "huh-uh." Nodding or shaking your head cannot be preserved on the transcript.

- **Estimates and Guesses.** An "estimate" is a calculated approximation arrived at following considered thought.[20] This is permitted. A guess is a supposition or prediction without adequate information.[21] It is reckless to provide an answer anytime, much less in deposition, where you have no real information and are simply making something up to please the questioner. The common example used by many attorneys is that if you were asked the size of the conference table, you would be able to provide a reasonable estimate. However, if you were to be asked to describe the dining room table in the attorney's home, unless you had more information such as being inside the home, seeing a photo, or having third-party information, any description on your part would be a "guess."

- **Correcting the record.** You may interrupt the proceedings at any time to correct or more fully explain an earlier answer. Sometimes a question is answered within one context as you understood it at the time, but then, upon further questioning, it is apparent that the answer you gave earlier should have been different because you now understand a different context in which the question was asked. While any significant change in your testimony will give the opposing attorney a chance to impeach your testimony with the jury, it is more important that the information in your final deposition is as accurate as you can make it.

- **Transcript review.** A transcript of your testimony in booklet form will be provided to you at some later date (in most federal circuits, although not all). This will give you an opportunity to review your statements for accuracy. You may make all the changes you wish, including correcting misspelled or incorrect words. However, if you change a "yes" into a "no," or "red" into "blue," then the attorney may question you in court about the change. This could reflect poorly on your credibility with the jury.

---

[20] www.merriam-webster.com/dictionary/estimate.
[21] www.merriam-webster.com/dictionary/guess.

- **Breaks and consultation with your attorney.** You may ask for a break at any point in the deposition. It is not an endurance test. You may consult with your attorney, and you may refer to reports and transcripts from prior proceedings if you ask before doing so. However, once a question is asked, you must answer it before consulting with your attorney or taking the break.

A Tactical Choice Not to Provide Admonitions

There is a recent trend by attorneys to dispense with the admonitions altogether, choosing to address testimony issues during the deposition as they arise. The attorneys' reasoning is that there is nothing in the state or federal rules of evidence requiring them to admonish you about your testimony. They believe the admonitions further train you to be a better witness against their client. Tactically, eliminating the admonitions provides them the opportunity to begin intensively questioning you immediately after introducing themselves. Admonishments give you time to settle down and orient to the procedure, and in their view, that is counter to their interests.

By reserving the admonitions until needed by a witness' testimony (e.g., saying "Uh-huh" instead of "Yes."), the attorney is able to interrupt the witness' flow, and, in effect, criticize while appearing to be "helpful." In the course of the first half-hour, interrupting and correcting a witness ten or more times, sometimes repeatedly, can lead to tentativeness in the testimony. Tentative witnesses are poor witnesses. This can only help his case against you.

By reading and understanding the admonitions listed in the previous section, you will be well prepared to deal with this attorneys' tactic. It is very likely your own attorney will also go over the admonitions prior to your deposition testimony. Keep them in mind as you prepare for the deposition, and while giving your testimony.

Objections

Some attorneys provide an admonition concerning objections by your attorney. Some do not and will simply wait until your attorney first objects. Objections are inevitable and they can throw off the unwary deponent who was not advised of the practice the first time it happens. However, like objections during criminal trials, you should stop talking until the objection is stated. The difference with the deposition is that a judge is not present to rule on whether you are required to answer the question or not. In the deposition, once the objection(s) is stated, you will answer the question unless your attorney directs you otherwise.

The reason you usually have to answer the Plaintiff's attorney's questions over your attorney's objections is that the judge will rule on admissibility at a later time. This "preserves the record," permitting your attorney to later object to the same question in court and have its admissibility ruled on by the judge. Failing to object to any question during the deposition is tantamount to your attorney agreeing that it is a proper question and should be answered.

There may be an objection to an entire line of questioning. The objection may be "standing," meaning it is on-going for the entire subject the opposing attorney is pursuing. By making a standing objection, your attorney preserves the right to object to the question in court without having to interrupt the flow of questioning by saying, "Objection!" and then providing the basis for the objection after every question. This quickly becomes tedious, and the standing objection saves a lot of time while allowing everyone to keep a continuity of thought.

You may be directed by your attorney not to answer a particular question or series of questions. This instruction is given when there is protected information the Plaintiff's attorney is not legally entitled to. Opposing attorneys generally attempt to sneak improper questions into the direct examination in the hopes of getting information they are not permitted to have that may give them an advantage. To be fair, many believe they actually do have a right to that information. Follow your attorney's direction and refuse to answer. Some officers are hesitant about not answering, fearing they may be courting trouble. This is a procedural question, and will by no means cause you to be "in contempt of court."

This question will be marked by the court reporter and the two attorneys will fight it out in front of the judge at a later date. Sometimes the Plaintiff's attorney will make a loud threat to "call the judge and have him rule on the question right now," with the arguments flying back and forth, the shouting gaining in intensity and volume, and the tone getting more and more personal. It is all fine drama. Sit back, watch, and take the time to wonder that a person in an adult body can act in such a manner and still be called a "professional." It's rare that the phone call to the judge is actually made, and business will usually get back to normal soon after the theatrics.

Generally the judge will later rule on its admissibility. Depending upon the Plaintiff's attorney's perception of whether or not your sworn answer to that question is vital to his case, you may be required to give an additional deposition to provide the information. Again, follow your attorney's advice.

Objections as Red Flags During Testimony

Pay attention to reasons given during your attorney's objections. The best advice is to follow his lead. When the objection is simply, "lacks foundation," "assumes facts not in evidence," and, "cumulative; asked and answered," simply proceed with your answer. However, there are other objections that should give you the signal that you are now in a minefield and your answer could blow up on you:

"Incomplete hypothetical." You may be given a hypothetical scenario to answer (this is very similar to what many experience in their hiring or promotional interviews, where you are expected to answer "what you would do if..."). The opposing attorney will provide you with perhaps two or three factors and then ask you to respond with how you would react or behave. If your attorney objects with an "incomplete hypothetical" argument, this should alert you to the fact that you don't have enough information to answer the question—the opposing counsel has not provided sufficient context in his question and it is out of context. This may be purposeful in an attempt to mislead you, or it may be innocent. In any case, answering something without the proper contextual foundation will *always* be bad for you.

Because the limited scenario provided is similar to the fact pattern of the present case, officers will often leap to answer, giving the same reasoning they employed during the incident. BEWARE: incomplete hypotheticals permit the opposing attorney to manufacture improper conduct within the current case.

Your response to the question after this type of objection might be:

- "I'm sorry, but I don't have enough information to give you an answer."

- You may even repeat back the facts as given and add more information that would create a reasonable belief or need to respond, creating a more complete hypothetical.

  o If the attorney stops you because those were not the facts he wanted you to consider, explain that you do not have sufficient information within the question he asked to be able to answer.

- If pressed, explain why there isn't enough information in the opposing attorney's scenario and why you cannot answer.

  o "I'm sorry, sir, but you asked the question with facts A, B, and C, and that isn't enough information for me to act upon. If, however, you add facts D and E, like I faced with your client's husband, then I would…"

"Vague." This signals there isn't enough information or specificity in the question to answer it well. Answering the question as put to you permits the opposing attorney and/or his expert to establish a context that you did not consider or assume. For example:

- "Isn't it true that striking a suspect in the head with a baton is prohibited?"

- "Isn't true that an officer is not permitted to shoot a suspect who just brandishes a knife?"

- "Isn't it true that officers are not permitted to punch a handcuffed prisoner?"

The proper answer to each question above is, "Sometimes. It depends on the context of each event, what the suspect is doing, and what the officer reasonably believes at the moment he makes the decision to respond."

"Vague as to time." This is a subset of the above objection. Your attorney will object because the question is generally about something you actually did, but with no specified time attached to the action. If you answer this question, your answer may be used out of context in the chronology of the event in an attempt to confuse either you or the jury as to when you made a decision or performed an act.

You may ask for the context or where in the timeline he is referring to, or you may elect to provide the proper context in your answer. Either way, the point on the timeline of your action or observation is crucial to its relevance—and ultimately its reasonableness—in your decision-making.

"In what circumstance?" This is a flag alerting you to the need to establish the context of the question before answering. In each instance, the totality of each of the circumstances will determine the reasonableness of the situation. Always provide your answer in the context you intend.

"Confusing." Asking a clear, clean question in deposition and trial is an art. Some attorneys are artists, and many others…well…are not. The pressure of the rules of evidence and the examination of a witness (you) combined with every word being transcribed sometimes commingle to make a torturous question that is impossible to understand. Add to all this pressure the financial consequences of a poor performance, and some attorneys seem to melt down many times within a single depo (and later in trial, which is not a bad thing for you when the Plaintiff's attorney keeps having to rephrase question after question because he cannot seem to put ten words together into an understandable phrase).

There will be other times your attorney may object because he wants you to think real hard about the question and to hear it again. When you hear this objection, ask for the question to be repeated even though you think you know what the question meant. Pay attention. Listen to the question with new ears and look for traps. Restate the question in your own words if you need to in order to keep it clear and accurate.

"Misstates testimony." This mistake may be innocent or it may be tactical. Some attorneys routinely misstate the evidence, purposely omitting the facts justifying your actions, beliefs, or response, or inserting "facts" that change the nature of the question or the event itself. In every case where the opposing attorney is restating your testimony, be extremely cautious about agreeing with his recounting of your testimony. If your attorney objects to the misstatement of the facts, ensure your answer is clear and based on the facts as you know them to be. Either ask for the question to be restated and clarify it with the proper facts, or simply give the facts as you know them to be in your answer.

- Note: Many attorneys who intentionally misstate an officer's testimony will throw a fit if the officer attempts to restate or change the question. You may hear, "Officer, I am directing you to answer the question as it is put to you," or, "…as I asked it." Follow your attorney's lead and don't play this game. If you cannot answer the question because it has incorrect information, say so. Never agree to anything that is not correct simply because the opposing attorney attempts to pressure you into it.

- You may also request the source of his quotation of your testimony and ask to review it before you confirm or deny what he just purported as the facts in the case.

When your attorney objects to a question, he may begin clarifying that question by adding facts or some factors that were missing. Again, look for the pattern or context he is setting for you. For example,

- "Objection. How are you (the opposing counsel) distinguishing between 'mentally ill,' 'mentally disabled,' and 'mentally impaired'? Because I just heard you use all three interchangeably."

  o If you do not have an exact definition for the words you are being asked about, or you are not permitted the opportunity to define the words, you are, again, in a minefield. Make sure you are answering the question the attorney is actually putting to you by asking for the attorney's definition of the word or phrase. Oftentimes, your request will result in the attorney asking you to define the word or phrase.

  o If you catch the opposing attorney using improper terms interchangeably, you may want to define the terms for the record to ensure there is no later misunderstanding or misuse of your testimony. Some opposing attorneys appreciate this clarification, others do not.

- "Objection. In addition to what he's (you) already said?"

  o This type of objection is in answer to a question where you have previously stated a number of reasons for your actions, and the opposing attorney is probably attempting to limit the factors and reasons for your response or decision-making. Include the entire list of reasons, facts, and circumstances upon which you relied at the scene in your answer. It is always a good idea to list every reason for each of these questions, no matter how many times you are asked—it helps to prevent your answer being taken out of context.

Attorney Mind-Games

Some attorneys will play games hoping to rattle you and get you off-balance. Some hope to push your buttons and cause you to become emotionally unsettled, or to react impulsively or emotionally. Some attempt to intimidate you with threats and dark insinuations. These attorneys become predictable and often have a negative reputation within the legal community. Even so, it is often disconcerting for officers who are unprepared for this unprofessional conduct and are walking into a deposition to give what, up to now, is the testimony of their lives.

Firearms in the deposition. If in plainclothes, the attorney will ask if you are currently armed. Whether the question is asked or you are openly carrying a handgun because you are in uniform or are displaying a badge, some attorneys will feign outrage that you are carrying a weapon into a "court proceeding" in an attempt to intimidate the Plaintiff(s)/Plaintiff's attorney/both or all of them. He will then demand you take your weapon to your vehicle. If you rightfully refuse (and your attorney backs your refusal), the opposing lawyer may throw a tantrum while threatening to "call the judge for a ruling."

- Keep your cool. Recognize the game for what it is (weak). Always follow your counsel's advice.

- Follow your policy. Some agencies have policies that do not permit the unlocked storage of a firearm in a personal vehicle. If your policy does not permit you to lock your loaded weapon in your vehicle, notify your attorney. If your attorney wishes to continue with the deposition as scheduled, phone your direct supervisor or agency legal liaison to notify them of the situation and to seek their guidance.

Threats of perjury or criminal prosecution. The Plaintiff's attorney will wait until he is on the record, will introduce himself, and then will announce some form of the following:

- "Just for the record, and I think it is only fair to warn you that I will be forwarding the transcript of this deposition to the federal prosecutor for an investigation into a charge of perjury against you in this case. I did this in a case a few years ago against two officers from (a jurisdiction somewhere in your state). They were both charged with perjury and convicted of a felony for which they went to prison. I just thought I should warn you before we begin."

Another attorney starts off his depositions in shooting cases where the suspect was killed by stating:

- "I will be forwarding this testimony and the evidence of this case to the federal prosecutor for an investigation into your murder of my client's husband/son/father, and your criminal violation of his civil rights. I will not rest until you are in prison. I did this a few years ago against two officers who were successfully prosecuted and imprisoned…"

Attorneys who make these threats are simply bullies. They also tend to truly believe that "all cops lie" and in the existence of "the code of silence" and "The Thin Blue Lie." One plaintiff's attorney employed the same "…*two officers a couple of years ago…*" threat for the last fifteen years of his career. These scare tactics might work if you are planning on lying or had actually murdered or beaten a subject for no justifiable reason. However, you have the facts of the case, your reasonable conduct, your training and experience, and your integrity on your side. You know you did a good job, and having forewarning about this plaintiff's "attorney's game," you should have an edge in dealing with the fear and intimidation this type of attorney seeks use against you.

Rudeness. Some attorneys are incredibly and, sometimes, shockingly rude. Some use it as a tactic in an attempt to gain an advantage. Many exhibiting this type of behavior are simply being who they are. Both types are attempting—and perhaps expecting—to punch your buttons and cause you to become emotionally hooked into their game. They may even hope you lose your temper. Don't let it happen. If you lose your temper or are rude in return, the jury will translate your behavior into the following belief: *if you are rude in a courtroom where you have no control, how rude must you be on the street where you are the authority?*

Be the professional you are. Do not expect the Plaintiff's attorney to be nice to you. If you need a friend, buy a dog. And don't react to the provocation, no matter how low he goes (and some go unbelievably low).

Arrogant smart-aleck. Some officers don't respond well to the arrogance exhibited by opposing counsel. This blatant disrespect for you and the truth regarding an incident where you were assaulted by his client can cause some defendant officers to become sarcastic in return. While juries generally react negatively to a smart-ass, arrogant attorney, they will punish an officer who exhibits the same negative qualities. Again, the juror's rationale is simple: *if you are a jerk in court where you are accused of misconduct, then you must have been a total jerk in the street where you had the power with nothing restraining your conduct.*

Be respectful and restrained in the face of disrespect. You will appear to be far stronger and much more professional than going mano-a-mano (or, rather, ego-a-ego) against the opposing attorneys. Just a suggestion you might want to take to heart.

Be respectful and restrained in the face of disrespect. You will appear to be far stronger and much more professional than going mano-a-mano (or, rather, ego-a-ego) against the opposing attorneys. Just a suggestion you might want to take to heart.

Your sympathetic, new best friend. While some are incredibly rude or arrogant, other plaintiffs' attorneys are amazingly gracious. The *single attorney* like this I worked against is a very, very nice man who is an incredibly smart and dangerous plaintiffs' attorney. Even the attorney I was working with told me how nice this gentleman was. It was the most pleasurable disagreement I have ever experienced as I pointed out that it was reasonable, given the totality of the facts known to the officers at the time, for the officers to have shot and killed his client's son. And I had to remind myself during the deposition that, "This man is not my friend."

Others use this as a ploy, apparently agreeing with nearly everything you say—until they suddenly don't. You will be talking away, chatting on and on while explaining to an apparently sympathetic listener who seems to be interested only in your side of the case, nodding at your every explanation when—*wham!*—Mr. Sympathetic disappears and Mr. Hardcase suddenly appears out of nowhere. It's like a schizophrenic

"Good-Cop/Bad-Cop" scenario as the mild-mannered Dr. Jekyll transforms into Mr. Hyde without warning. While it is much more pleasant to be questioned by someone like this, it apparently makes it easy for some officers to forget that they are in an adversarial situation. When they are abruptly reminded by this type of ambush, some become seemingly and irrevocably rattled.

This person is not your new best friend. He wants to make a lot of money through an adverse judgment based on the answers you are giving as he smiles and nods his head. If he wins, this will be a very public record of your work history and a damning commentary on your competence. He may be a really nice guy. *She* may be a very attractive young woman who smiles sweetly and is so very attentive and interested in every word you say.

While he or she might be a "nice person" in a different setting, or even someone you would like to know, remember this: that attorney would likely slit your throat to win this case. Keep your friends close, and your enemies closer. If you begin feeling comfortable in your deposition because of the collegial atmosphere created by the attorney, you are simply acting your role as the lamb being led to slaughter.

The best advice: Stay frosty, focusing on your mission. Remain adversarial in a professional manner, and remember that no one sitting on the other side of the table is your buddy. That goes for the court reporter as well—he or she is being paid by the Plaintiff's attorney, and may have unknown loyalties from years of being employed by him for depositions.

Attorney Tricks

Some attorneys believe that being a litigator is about tricking the other person into saying something damaging rather than simply allowing the facts and circumstances of the case to speak for themselves. These attorneys count on officers not keeping up to speed with their agency's policies and the current laws regarding the seizure of persons and force. They also count on your being nervous, anxious, and unsure of the facts of the case, having not *studied* the case, including your written narrative reports and the transcripts of any interviews you may have provided.

These attorneys can be defeated through your careful preparation prior to the deposition. The tricks and methods they use can take the form of the following:

Non-sequential questioning. The reasonableness of your actions and every force response is based on the context—the totality of the facts known to you at the time—forced upon you by the suspect's decisions and behavior. The timeline of the events also matter a great deal. While many attorneys ask you to walk them through the incident and will ask questions about specific matters after you have completed the chronology of the event, others take a different tack. These professionals will do everything they can to keep you from answering questions in sequence and chronological order. Seemingly every question they ask is out of context. This type of attorney specializes in mixing up the timeline in an attempt to confuse or manipulate you into making errors in your testimony.

This non-cohesive jumble of testimony is designed to keep you off-balance. Over time, the attorney knows you will fatigue and let down your guard, especially if you are not prepared for it.

If your attorney is competent, you will likely hear many objections regarding "vague as to time," "confusing," and "Clarification. Did you mean X or did you mean Y with that last question?" Even assuming you are working with a sharp civil defense attorney, there is still a level at which you must fend for yourself and protect your case. There are at least two ways of handling this:

- Ask the attorney questioning you to restate the question and, if you are not given an indication of when in the case timeline he's asking about, ask for clarification. Asking, "When are you referring to?" is always appropriate.

- State when this particular event happened so that the context is in your answer. For instance, "I drew my TASER with my left hand immediately after Mr. Smith drew his knife out of what was later determined to be a sheath on his right rear hip while screaming at me, 'I'm going to cut your head off and piss down your throat!'" For some depositions, each of your answers will have to be like this, providing the event(s) that occurred just before the subject of the question, and the event(s) that immediately followed so that your answer is in and of itself independent of the question, and is in context within the chronology of the event. It makes for a long deposition, but also provides an accurate one when forced to deal with this type of questioning.

"...isn't that correct, Officer?" You were alerted earlier in this text to the fact that some attorneys are incredibly skilled at the game of "misstatement." And others believe they are incredibly skilled at it when, in fact, they are not. The phrase, "...isn't that correct?" or some variation should warn you that statement is very likely a set-up and could very well be a misstatement of facts or previous testimony.

This misstatement can end with a variation of a question that fundamentally asserts, "...isn't that correct?" Or the question may begin, "Isn't it true..." When you hear any version of this phrase, that red light that just began furiously flashing in the corner of your eye is warning you that you are being set up, so you had better think carefully about what he just said. It is likely the opposing attorney just left out the key component that justifies your actions and/or response.

In civil court, you are responsible for knowing and understanding everything you have testified to or reported from the first moment you heard the dispatched information or saw the on-view crime.

You may hear a statement that is purported to represent a correct recitation of your previous testimony in this or prior cases. In a civil case, you likely have a lot of prior testimony to keep track of. The same thing may have been stated in different ways at different times, although the meaning remained the same and conveyed the same content, but only *within that context* as it was presented at the time. In civil court, you are responsible for knowing and understanding everything you have testified to or reported from the first moment you heard the dispatched information or saw the on-view crime. If you knew or had repeated contacts with the deceased or plaintiff, you will be held responsible for that testimony as well.

In some cases, you may have:

- Provided a written narrative report (including a separate "use of force" report and various supplemental reports).

- Testified in the prosecution of the Plaintiff in front of a criminal jury.

- Testified before a grand jury.

- Been required to provide one or more interviews for your Internal Affairs or Professional Standards Unit.

- Signed Interrogatories (as part of the discovery process, Interrogatories are a series of questions developed by opposing counsel and answered by the parties in the case under penalty of perjury).

The attorney will also likely ask you detailed questions about your training in:

- The laws regarding force, search and seizure, impounding vehicles, etc.

- Your agency policy(ies).

- Your agency's/academy's/state's training standards.

The cleverest attorneys will set you up with more finesse. These professionals will provide you with complete, correct, and proper information in their questions as they ask time after time:

- "…isn't that correct?"

- "…isn't that what you saw?"

- "And officer, you would agree that…"

Until they don't. Like a well-trained high-pressure salesman or a good police interrogator, this type of attorney gets you in the habit of saying, "Yes." Psychologists tell us that people want to say yes, and most feel guilty when they say "No." Especially if the individual has been working on you, setting you up to say, "Yes," after you have already said "yes" a number of times is succession.

Witnesses, including officers, are sometimes naïve in their assumptions that attorneys should not be able to mislead or lie in court. Being mentally focused for ten minutes is relative easy for most people. Maintaining that sharp focus for three, five, and even seven hours of intensive, hostile questioning is tiring. Tired people relax, daydream, and cease paying attention. Attorneys know that, and count on that normal human lapse.

Taking a break every hour or two is a good idea.

Take frequent breaks. Have to use the bathroom? Ask to take a break. Getting a bit worn down and fuzzy? Ask to take a break. Taking a bit of a beating? Ask to take a break and disrupt his tempo. Taking a break every hour or two is a good idea. It gives the court reporter a break, and this will be appreciated. It permits you to get up, use the restroom, talk to your attorney, make a phone call, or just let your guard down for a few minutes.

Officers sometimes have trouble with this type of questioning because what the attorney is asking "sort of sounds like something I heard at some training I attended somewhere a few years ago." Unsure, defendant officers often agree when they shouldn't. The following questions are some glaring misstatements that officers, sergeants, administrators, and even chiefs of police and sheriffs have erroneously agreed to after an attorney stated, "I am going to ask you about your understanding of your training regarding the laws you enforce":

1. "If an officer is losing a fight, or underestimates the suspect's ability, that officer's ability to successfully control a suspect is greatly impaired without the use of increased or excessive force in order to get the situation under control, isn't that right?"

2. "Isn't it true that you were trained that case law has held that deadly force can only be used in response to deadly force or in situations where there is a threat of serious physical harm?"

3. "Officers are instructed in the academy and during their career to escalate the amount of force they are using to the amount of force used against them, matching the force presented by the suspect, isn't that your understanding?"

4. "It's true, is it not, that the escalation of the level of force by a police officer causes or allows the suspect to also escalate his level of force?

5. "An officer is trained that deadly force is only reasonable when the suspect is attempting to kill you with a deadly weapon, isn't that right, Officer?"

Possible answers to the questions might be:[22]

1. "No, sir. Excessive force by police is never permitted. If I am losing a fight, I have been trained that I may respond with objectively reasonable force, up to and including deadly force, in order to defend my life or that of another's, to effect an arrest, to overcome resistance, and to prevent escape. Just because I was losing a fight, and then fought back with the means and intensity of force sufficient to overcome the advantage the suspect had through his violence does not mean I resorted to excessive force."

2. "No, sir. While I may respond with deadly force in the face of an actual and immediate deadly threat, I am also able to justifiably act upon my reasonable belief that I am in imminent threat (about to occur), even though my reasonable belief is later found to be wrong or mistaken. I am trained that case law permits me, as an officer, to make reasonable mistakes, even when that mistake results in the

---

[22] Check the current force law in your state and federal district.

death of someone who was innocently behaving in a way that I reasonably misunderstood to be threatening."

3. "No, sir. I was trained that officers are able to overcome the suspect's violence with force that is reasonably proportionate and with greater injury potential than that of the offender's. For example, I may employ a TASER or OC spray against a suspect who is threatening to fight with me. I may also employ a Police Service Dog or baton to overcome the empty-hand assault by the subject who is punching at me. If the subject attempts to use a baseball bat to injure me, I may legally and reasonably respond with deadly force. 'Matching force' is force law for civilians, not the police."

4. "No, sir. Offenders may not legally resist an officer's lawful arrest. If the officer responds with reasonable force to overcome the suspect's resistance, the offender may not escalate in return and resist with a more injurious degree or type of force. The offender is obligated by law to submit to arrest."

5. "No, sir. Officers may respond with deadly force when they have an objective and reasonable belief that their life, or that of another's, is in actual or imminent danger of death or serious bodily injury, based on the totality of the facts known to the officer at the time. If my reasonable belief is that I am about to die or be seriously injured, and I no longer expect or believe that I can continue the fight because of injuries or fatigue, I may respond with deadly force to stop the fight regardless of whether or not the suspect is armed with a weapon."

Accusations of "conspiracy" and "cover-ups." Many Plaintiffs' attorneys are convinced that all cops lie and that they will cover for each other. They will ask you accusingly about the "Code of Silence" and, "Isn't it true that it is common for officers to routinely cover up misconduct by other officers?" The attorney will indirectly accuse you of conspiracy and cover-up, asking about the "common practice" of the "Thin Blue Lie" and "testi-lying." They always have a story about some officers sometime in the past in a case this attorney handled who colluded together to obstruct justice and deny the plaintiff his rightful recovery of damages. In the mind of these attorneys, it is often prima facie evidence of conspiracy and cover-up when involved officers and witness officers relate the same relative fact pattern about the events at the scene. Because the officers are telling the same story, it is therefore proof to this attorney the officers are colluding. They literally cannot fathom that two or more officers effectively testifying and relating the facts of the case are telling the truth as they honestly believe them to be.

Be prepared to explain that while you have heard of this practice of the Code of Silence in the past and in the media, that is not your experience of policing. The idea of not tolerating misconduct and then perjuring one's self to protect malicious officers is best exemplified in the commonly heard police phrase, "I'm willing to die for you, but I won't lie for you."

Protect the Record

The deposition, as has previously been explained, is for dual purposes: the first, to get your sworn testimony memorialized on the record for the proceeding, and second, to gain information in order to attack your credibility and veracity. Your job, in support of giving the most accurate, truthful testimony you can possibly provide, is to protect the transcript of the proceedings.

A few minutes into the deposition, in all likelihood, it will feel as if you are being intensely interrogated by the opposing counsel. After an hour of going back and forth, explaining yourself and your reasons for your actions during the incident, your butterflies and anxiety are history, and you are simply giving testimony. At some point over the next few hours, you will likely be asked to view a diagram of the scene, photos, or some other kind of evidence. You will be asked questions about what you are viewing and explaining. You may be asked about some physical action, such as what the suspect did with his hand, or how you reached over to take hold of the suspect.

NEVER FORGET THE COURT REPORTER. She is taking down your oral answers. She will not describe for the record exactly where you pointed on the diagram of the scene to one of the many automobiles parked on the street, or to which of the six people standing on a street corner in a still photo taken from a surveillance camera. This all-important transcript of your testimony will not enable the reader to understand what you meant when you said, "Here." "This one." "Right there." "Yup, behind that one." The best that reader will get from a transcript in this situation is one that reads, "'Here,' (indicating)." This tells the reader nothing other than you pointed somewhere or indicated some movement.

When you are asked to point something out, describe in detail what you are talking about: "On photo numbered Bates Stamp 0328, there is the suspect vehicle on the left, the red Ford F150, with my police vehicle parked behind it. The subject stepped from behind this tree, the one immediately to the left of the Ford shown in this photo—here (indicating). I first saw an object in his right-hand when he stepped toward his driver's door. After a couple of steps, I was able to identify the object as a handgun when the suspect was approximately two or three steps away from the driver's side of his vehicle...Um, right here" as you point it out to the attorneys in the conference room.

Tedious? Absolutely. But if someone had photo 0328 in his hand three to six months later, and he wanted to know when the deposed officer had first seen and then identified that now-very important object in the right hand, or he wanted to know more than, "She moved like this," a full explanation of the movement would give a better understanding than if you had simply said, "Uh...here," or, "Um, like this," with the Plaintiff's attorney replying, "OK," before moving on with the next question.

If you are asked to describe movement, it may sound something like, "After I repeatedly ordered whoever was inside the bathroom to open the door, I kicked it with my right foot. Because there was no electrical power to the apartment, there was no light in the room except from that coming from several small holes in the exterior wall. I saw a woman in a t-shirt and panties squatting in front of the bathtub with both of her hands inside the waistband of her underwear. She was looking up, directly at me. I ordered her to get on the floor, but she suddenly stood up to about, oh, three-quarters of the way to full standing position, with her legs still bent, like she was crouching. As she stood up, she pulled her hands out of her waistband to about here, just about to her naval. I could see she was clutching something, but her left hand hid it from view. It was dark in the windowless bathroom. I told her to slowly show me what she had in her hands. That's when she punched her right hand at me like this, right at my face with her arm extended, her hand in a fist and I saw a flash in the darkness that looked like a gun barrel…"

Without this specificity in your deposition testimony, the Plaintiff's attorney, who may accurately remember what you said or not, or who may be intentionally attempting to mislead the jury, could indicate some action or movement other than your actual demonstration. This creates another point to argue, and another possible doubt in the mind of the jury as to what your testimony actually was.

Protect yourself and your case by scrupulously protecting the record.

In a deposition, the record—the transcript—is everything. Clearly say "yes" or "no," don't step on the attorney's questions, and don't point at a photograph or diagram and say, "Here," or replicate a movement by saying, "Like this," without creating a word picture for the court reporter to record in the transcript. Protect yourself and your case by scrupulously protecting the record.

The Stipulation

At some point you will hear the longed for words, "I have no further questions." You're done and about to be released from the deposition. Time to let down a bit, but do not tune out just yet. While fatigued, your adrenaline is likely still a factor in your physical and emotional condition.

The attorneys will come to an agreement, or if this is not the first deposition in this case, they will have already agreed how they want the deposition to be handled from this point. You will then hear them "stipulate," or state an agreement for the record.

Within that agreement, the attorneys agree whether or not you will be permitted to review and correct the record (this may not be available to you in your state or circuit court). Generally you will be permitted this review and correction, and will be required to return it to your attorney within an agreed upon number of days.

If you are given the option of reading your testimony and making any needed corrections, ALWAYS OPT TO REVIEW AND CORRECT YOUR TESTIMONY. While any of your changes may open the door to question your truthfulness and credibility, it is always better to have your testimony be as accurate as possible for the record. This deposition testimony will be used to compare against your trial testimony. Any discrepancies in your court testimony will be pointed out to the jury. Be cautious about the changes and corrections. The more glaring any individual error in your original testimony and/or a high number of serious discrepancies, the more likely the jury may disbelieve your account of the incident and side with the Plaintiff.

Once you have reviewed your testimony and made any corrections, you will sign the deposition in the space provided. This certifies under penalty of perjury that the testimony contained in the deposition is accurate and represents your truthful recall of the facts expected in your future testimony.

About Reviewing and Correcting Your Depo

Correcting your deposition is something that should be performed with caution. Any substantive changes, such as changing a "Yes" into a "No" can have huge ramifications to your court testimony. Feel free to correct spelling or incorrectly transcribed words. However, have a solid, articulable reason for any changes to the record. You will very likely be intensively questioned about these changes.

"Errata form." You will likely be provided with an "errata" form at the end of the deposition booklet. You may use that form for simple word changes. The errata form is a table where you note page and line numbers, what the incorrect word(s) or phrase(s) to be struck out is, and the corrected word or language to be substituted. This form will be supplied to the Plaintiff's attorney so that he may be apprised of the changes to the transcript of your testimony.

If you are not provided with an errata form, it is easy to create your own table and fill it in. In the example below, there are three columns labeled: "Page/Line," "Text to be Deleted," and "Insert Corrected Text."

Page/Line	Text to be Deleted	Insert Corrected Text
15/22	West	East
44/2	He shouted, "Get out of here."	He shouted, "Get out of here," as he reached for the handgun lying on the chest of drawers to his left.

Be sure to sign and date the form. Whether you print by hand or supply your own generated errata sheet, it is your responsibility to ensure it is legible.

LEGIBILY write the corrections in the deposition booklet itself by hand in blue or black ink. Cross out the incorrect testimony with a single line, leaving it legible. Then insert the correct language or word(s) in the margins or between sentences (deposition transcripts are often double-spaced). Ensure the inserted words or language is clearly legible. And initial each change.

Your corrected copy is the deposition your attorney will likely refer to during trial. By making these changes in the body of the deposition itself, it will aid him in using your proper testimony rather than having to remember to accurately cite the information contained in your errata form.

Chapter Four Summary:

This deposition will set up your testimony in the civil trial in front of the jury. This is your chance to provide solid, accurate, and very importantly, comprehensive information about your decision-making, actions, behavior, and that of your fellow officers relative to the suspect's behavior and action at the time of the incident.

- This testimony is different than anything you have likely experienced during criminal prosecution testimony. It is exacting, thorough, detailed, often seemingly—or actually—redundant, and prolonged. It is also the result of a multi-year process where you have likely provided testimony and written narratives multiple times, offering an opportunity to compare each instance of your reporting of the facts in the case.

- Preparing for your deposition should be deliberate, comprehensive, and undertaken with the same attitude as preparing for an important test. If your preparation for a sergeant's exam is lackadaisical and sloppy, your test results will likely reflect that preparation. Like any examination of your knowledge, if you take the time to know the case material until you are conversant in it, the deposition transcript will serve you well as the blueprint for your testimony in front of the jury in the courtroom.

- Your efforts will very likely mean the difference between a successful deposition assisting the defense of your actions, and supporting a summary judgment. A poor deposition may not only destroy your chances for a summary judgment, but can create huge problems for your later court testimony and the resulting judgment.

Understanding how the deposition is conducted provides you a context for your testimony preparations. The better you prepare, the more likely you'll have a desirable outcome at trial.

CHAPTER FIVE

The Last Word

Professionalism in law enforcement is measured in many ways, some more meaningful than others. Standing on the street being sworn at by an individual while you maintain quiet restraint, arresting without incident an individual who brutalized a child or murdered a cop, or finally getting a violently resistive suspect into handcuffs without any retaliatory force even though he injured you, are just a few of many examples of professional conduct. You do this because you are a cop, a professional law enforcement officer.

Professional standards are not solely measured in the street. They are also measured in your post-force actions, those required to prove your proper conduct. This includes your first report or interview, the Professional Standards investigation interview, and perhaps testimony in a coroner's inquest or a grand jury. Next in line is your upcoming deposition. The extent of your professionalism will be coolly judged and in great detail based on your comportment in both the deposition and the court room, how well you articulate the facts as you perceived them, and how those perceptions led to your reasonable beliefs as well as the manner in which you acted upon them.

By now, you understand that your decision-making and actions will be scrutinized to a degree you likely have never experienced before. You are entering into a world of arcane rules where you have no control other than over your own emotions and ability to testify.

If you take the time to prepare, you will almost assuredly limit the time and number of questions you will be subjected to. A maximum of two or three questions per topic and a total of five minutes of exploration of your job knowledge and training is a serious win for you. One officer who made a dedicated effort to study and prepare for his testimony left his deposition believing all that study time was "wasted" because the opposing attorney asked him "just a few questions" about his core job knowledge before moving on to the facts of the case. Contrary to his beliefs, a review of his answers to those "few questions" showed a competency and professional knowledge that the opposing attorney quickly realized would provide no fertile ground for his efforts, and rapidly abandoned those lines of questioning. That preparation further paid off when that officer faced no questions in front of the jury about his job knowledge from the Plaintiff's attorney.

If you take the time to prepare, you will almost assuredly limit the time and number of questions you will be subjected to.

That's the point. Preparing well for the inevitable battle makes the battle easier to win and much less costly. Every warrior knows that if he or she cannot avoid a war, an easy win is the best fight of all. Easy wins result from a maximum effort in meaningful preparation. Easy wins are the best because you know it is a result of your effort.

Your preparation for this process should look very much like your preparation for a promotion that you really want. Your policies, the laws surrounding the events of the case, how you were trained, the facts of the case as you and others remember them, what the opposing expert is saying, and where the opposing attorney is attempting to convince the jury that you violated his client's civil rights, all require mastery from you. Studying until you begin dreaming about the material will not be wasted time.

Sitting in deposition, and later in court, struggling to explain, your testimony being contradicted and corrected throughout by the record of your past testimony, and slugging it out with the opposing attorney is not only exhausting, but damages your credibility as a professional in the eyes of the juror. It can also harm your self-confidence and leave you questioning yourself, sometimes for years. The civil process can traumatize the ill-prepared. It's just a fact.

It is up to you and the level of effort you are willing to put into this pre-deposition process that will largely determine your success. You are going into battle. There is no getting out of it, no wishing it would go away, no avoiding the reality that you will be center stage in a courtroom and accused of misconduct. This process can leave you feeling beat up and ill-prepared, or thinking it was easy, or, at least, "not that bad." That is wholly up to you.

So dig in. Prepare. Take this process seriously and go the extra mile. It will pay off for you professionally and help preserve your reputation. You know what you have to do. The question is, are you willing to put in the time and effort for the added benefits it will bring? It's not hard, it just takes hard work. Good luck.

Glossary of Terms

Admonitions. These are instructions and cautionary rules of the deposition explained to the deponent. Essentially, they are instructions to the witness on how to be a witness in this proceeding. Their purpose is to ensure the orderly progression of the deposition, and they vary greatly between attorneys. Some attorneys spend a great deal of time explaining every detail of "proper witness behavior," while others dispense with it completely.

Complaint for Damages and Demand for Jury Trial. This is the initial explanation of the plaintiff's case, his version of the facts, and the specific allegations of violation(s) of the plaintiff's rights by the defendant.

Consensual Contact. Known also as a "social contact," this is a non-enforcement contact by an officer with a citizen in which the officer is not exercising his police authority or force to stop or detain the subject. The citizen is free to disregard the presence of the officer and to decline or terminate a search (Florida v. Bostick, 501 U.S. 429, 111 S. Ct. 2382, (1991)).

Continuum of Force. This is a discredited training theory that was adopted by law enforcement as a short-cut in training officers how to respond with force given the behavior and perceived threat of a suspect. Variously pictured as a ladder, stair-steps, thermometer, and other creative concepts, its flaw is that it is the type of mechanistic solution the US Supreme Court warned against in Graham v. Connor. It is also referred to as a "Linear Force Continuum" because, unlike enforcement contacts resulting in a force response, the continuums envision a fight as a linear progression from "low to high" and require officers to "escalate" or "deescalate" progressively rather than simply responding to their reasonable perceptions of threat. It has been increasingly discarded by law enforcement policy developers and law enforcement trainers in favor of policy and training content based upon case law as applied to the incidents officers respond to.

Control. The phrase, "Control is something the suspect cedes to the officer," was coined by Thomas V. Benge, Sergeant of Police (retired).

Creating the Conditions (leading to force). This is a plaintiffs' concept that officers are able to intentionally manipulate the situation and thereby the actions of the suspect/plaintiff. The police action or tactic then causes the suspect to act in some manner the police can use as an excuse to harm the suspect. Examples of this are the "Split-Second Syndrome" (where officers intentionally position themselves too closely to the suspect to provide themselves reaction time, leading to perceptual mistakes such as thinking a cell phone is a gun, resulting in a shooting of an unarmed individual) or crowding a subject (the officer intentionally was rude to the subject and then intentionally crowded the subject, causing the individual to put his hands on the officer and push the officer away). It can also be related in some federal circuits to failing to articulate the basis of detaining or arresting the plaintiff.

Cushion of Safety. The concept of the "cushion of safety" is a Plaintiff's theory resulting from training regarding calls for service involving the mentally ill. Officers are legitimately trained "to avoid unnecessarily crowding the mentally ill subject." The mentally ill subject is already in distress (which is why he is being contacted by the police). Fear and confusion due to the disruption of coherent thought is the norm for a subject experiencing a psychotic break, and officers are trained that being too close and crowding the subject may cause the individual to lash out in a defensive reaction.

This is translated by the Plaintiff's expert to mean any action taken by the police to restrict the movement of the mentally ill subject, or any position taken by the contact-officer in communicating with the subject, and is just one of the causative factors of this police-caused force event which violated the subject's rights. The cushion-of-safety theory is a perfect mechanism for criticizing police conduct because the necessary distance for a sufficient "cushion" is ill defined, making any distance the officer chooses to be a "serious" error. Any attempt to set up a perimeter on an armed subject (e.g., knife) to prevent his moving toward uninvolved civilians will be a violation of the "cushion of safety" because it is always too close, regardless of the distance between the officer(s) and the subject.

Defendant. The individual (or corporation, including an incorporated city, state, or federal government) against whom a lawsuit is brought in a court of law.

Deponent. The individual giving sworn testimony during a deposition.

Discovery. A process by which each party to the lawsuit discloses and exchanges all of the facts, documents, witnesses, evidence, etc., to each other, via their attorneys. This prevents surprises in court, or "trial by ambush."

Errata Form. An "errata form" is employed to notify opposing counsel of errors in your testimony or in transcription of your testimony. "Errata" is the plural form of Latin meaning the correction of a document or book. The suggested form provides a record of the location (page and line number), the incorrect text or text to be corrected, and the corrected text you wish to have formally recognized for the record of your testimony.

Excessive Force. Per Black's Law Dictionary, "Force which cannot be justified in light of all the circumstances" (known to the officer at the time).

Expert Witness Rule 26 Report. FRCP §26(a)(2)(B) *Witnesses who must provide a written report.* Unless otherwise stipulated or ordered by the court, this disclosure must be accompanied by a written report - prepared and signed by the witness - if the witness is one retained or specially employed to provide expert testimony in the case or one whose duties as the party's employee regularly involve giving expert testimony. The report must contain: (i) a complete statement of all opinions the witness will express and the basis and reasons for them; (ii) the facts or data considered by the witness in forming them; (iii) any exhibits that will be used to summarize or support them; (iv) the witness's qualifications, including a list of all publications authored in the previous 10 years; (v) a list of all other cases in which, during the previous 4 years, the witness testified as an expert at trial or by deposition; and (vi) a statement of the compensation to be paid for the study and testimony in the case.

Incomplete Hypothetical. A "hypothetical" is a series of supposed or theoretical facts upon which a witness is to rely as the basis of their answer. An "incomplete hypothetical" is a list of facts that are not sufficient to permit the witness to come to a reasonable decision or opinion.

Interrogatories. Written answers to written questions signed under penalty of perjury as part of the discovery process.

Plaintiff. The party who initiates or brings a lawsuit in a court.

Plaintiffs' Bar. Licensed attorneys who specialize in plaintiffs' lawsuits. In the context of this book, it refers to attorneys who specialize in bringing suit against police officers and their agencies.

Probable Cause. A set of facts leading a reasonable and prudent person to believe the accused had committed a crime.

Reasonable Officer Standard. Generally defined as: "Would another officer with like or similar training and experience given the same or similar circumstances react in the same way or make similar decisions?" California POST Basic Course Workbook Series, Learning Domain 20, 2009. Page 16.

Reasonable Suspicion. It can be defined in several ways: "Facts that lead another to believe that criminal activity is afoot." Also, "Unusual or suspicious behavior related to a crime (that has occurred, is currently happening, or is about to occur) involving the person to be detained." It is not a "hunch," rather, a reasonable belief extracted from the facts known to the officer and drawn through his experience and training.

Stipulate. This is an explicit agreement about some point of argument or piece of evidence made by either or both of the attorneys. For example, if you were the involved officer in an officer-involved shooting and your bullet struck the suspect, your attorney will stipulate, or agree, that you shot the Plaintiff/Decedent, and this fact will not be a point of contention in the upcoming litigation.

Valid Core Transaction. This is simply fancy lawyer-speak for the manner in which you contacted the subject: consensual contact, detention, or probable cause arrest.

Case Law Cites

Scott v. Harris, 127 S.Ct. 1769 (2007)

Tennessee v. Garner, 105 S.Ct. 1694 (1985)

Graham v. Connor, 109 S.Ct. 1865 (1989)

Florida v. Bostick, 501 U.S. 429, 111 S. Ct. 2382, (1991)

Bryan v. McPherson, 590 F.3d 778 (9th Cir. 2009)

United States v. Richardson 208 F.3d 626, 630 (7th Cir. 2000)

Terry v. Ohio 392 U.S. 1, 88 S.Ct. 1868 (1968)

Be sure to consult with your local legal authority to ensure you are current with all legal and case law requirements.

About the Author

George T. Williams has been acting as a compensated expert witness since 1991. He is accepted nationwide as an expert in federal, state, and municipal courts, as well as in employment arbitration hearings. He provides testimony in many diverse areas of police litigation, including police force, deadly force, procedures, tactics, pursuits, Police Service Dog, patrol, SWAT, and jail cases.

Mr. Williams is a nationally and internationally known trainer and innovator of police force skills and programs including firearms, defensive tactics, impact weapons, aerosol restraint systems, arrest and control, and TASER (registered trademark). He routinely presents officer safety and survival classes nationwide, and has trained dozens of SWAT teams in his career. He is widely known for his civil liability prevention training, and ability to distill force law into applicable knowledge for the average officer.

A prolific author, Mr. Williams offers original thinking in police tactics and force response through his writing. He has authored over 200 articles in such prestigious publications as the FBI's "Law Enforcement Bulletin," the National Tactical Officers Association's "The Tactical Edge," the International Chiefs of Police "The Police Chief," "Law & Order," "The Police Marksman," the International Association of Law Enforcement Officers "The Firearms Instructor," and many more. His first book, "Force Reporting for Every Cop" (Jones and Bartlett, Boston, 2006), is a valuable tool in developing an officer's reporting skills.

To Contact the Author:

Email: gtwilliams@cuttingedgetraining.org
Website: http://www.cuttingedgetraining.org
LinkedIn: http://www.linkedin.com/profile/view?id=744327&
    trk=tab_pro
Facebook: http://www.facebook.com/pages/Cutting-Edge-
    Training-LLC/250387598425057

18573819R00071

Made in the USA
San Bernardino, CA
20 January 2015